Human-Dog Connection

Fantastic Creatures

When Handled With Love

If you treat your dog as if it is just a dog, that is what you will get. If you treat them like they are part of your family then a family member is what you will have.

Index

Chapter One
Deciding

Ch. Bifrost's I Like Ike "Ike"

There is a lot to consider before bringing a dog into the family. The human-dog connection is a very wonderful bond of loving energy and companionship. It is the human who makes it based in love or fear. Dogs have a great effect on our lives and we have the same effect on theirs. A dog is not to blame for the unacceptable behavior that they learned from the humans in their life. Humans are to blame if they feel the dog is making their life difficult in any way. Whatever behavior pattern the human is unhappy with, the dog, like a child, learned it from the humans in their life. A dog loves unconditionally. They will love you with all they have even if you physically hurt or neglect them. A dog that has not been taught positively will have fears. These fears will be reflected in their behavior.

A lot of books advise humans not to treat your dog like a human. To me that would depend on how you treat humans. Also, how do you treat a dog like a dog? Go around and smell their butts? Oh wait, no that would be acting like a dog. Staking them out in the yard? No, that would be treating them like a goat. Cage them up all the time? No, that would be treating them like chickens. Leave them loose in a fenced yard all the time? No, that would be treating them like a pony. When a dog fosters another species it raises it like a dog, not what it is. Dogs are the only species that can treat a dog like a dog.

If you believe dogs are inferior to humans, think about this. There are many things a dog can do that a human can not. Just because dogs cannot speak English does not make humans superior because they can. A dog, however, can learn any language you teach them. Can all humans learn to speak dog? Yes, they can. Just like humans, dogs can have jobs, Though they may not make money at their jobs, their jobs are very important. Some of these jobs cannot be done by humans. Can a human find another human under rubble, snow, or under water by just smelling? How many humans do you know who can smell out cancer or bed bugs? I could list different things dogs are capable of doing that humans are not, but I am sure humans are aware of them already. They are like any other family member in your household. Do they not deserve to be treated that way?

Let's compare it to the way someone might raise a child. If they allow their child to get away with everything they do wrong, then I say "no." Do not treat a dog like a human. If humans teach their children with unconditional love and understanding, I say "yes," treat a dog like a human.

Bringing a dog into the family is a commitment to caring for them until their body shuts down. Caring is not just food, water, and shelter. It includes teaching them with love and understanding.

In this book you will read about the mistakes humans make with dogs and how it affects a whole household. There is no such thing as a bad dog, just a dog that has not been taught differently. Would you consider a wild dog/wolf as having bad behavior? They do what they have to do to survive. Without human contact they survive. Humans are the ones who have the tendency to baby things and find behaviors as cute. Unfortunately dogs, do not know what is right and wrong to their human companion unless taught. If encouraged (encouraged…laughing or playing with) to do something as a puppy, they will learn this behavior pattern that will have to change as an adult. It is up to humans to provide for the dogs in the family. Think about it this way. The way your dog behaves today would they be able to go live with another family and not be tossed away due to their behavior? I have groomed many dogs that I feel most humans would not want to deal with in their home. I worked with every dog that I handled in my jobs. I showed/taught them that they had nothing to fear and I have to do whatever it is. The sad thing is more humans rid themselves of the dog instead of taking the time to **teach** them differently.

Giving away or dumping is definitely treating a dog like it is not human. It makes me wonder if these same humans had children and what they do with them when they continue to misbehave. I am sure they do not toss them out the door or give them to another human. Instead, they take the time to teach them differently with unconditional love and understanding. Is that considered treating a living creature like a human? I feel it is just treating a living creature humanely. Every living creature deserves to be treated humanely. Throughout this book I will compare situations where treating a dog like you might treat a child is the best way to prevent and change fearful behavior responses.

No matter what age the dog is, teaching will always be a part. "Can't teach old dogs new tricks" is not a fact. A dog at any age can get used to new patterns. Environment is the major factor in a dog's behavior. How they act is based on what they have learned from different experiences. They will adjust to changing locations and routines well if you teach them. It just takes time, patience and consistency.

Nature vs Nurture

I am sure you have heard the expression "nature vs nuture." This is very true when it comes to dogs and their behavior. Only a small bit of a dog's behavior can be linked to genetics (nature). A dog's behavior is based more on the way they are raised and what they experience (nurture). From the time a puppy's eyes and ears open they absorb all their experiences and learn different patterned behavioral responses to each. The humans reaction to their behavioral responses teaches the pattern behavior.

Puppies also learn from their canine mom and littermates loving and fearful behavior. A puppy raised by a barky dam learns the behavior is OK. SC Chihuahua "Tipper" came to my home at an older age and barked a lot with her get. Her daughters, "Ivy and Secret," learned very well that barking was normal until taught differently as they aged. If mom fears humans, the puppies will learn this. In cases like this, calm, loving human interaction with the puppies will decrease their fear.

"Tipper and Secret"

It is inhumane to get a puppy/dog (buy or adopt) and then just turn around and give it away. Bringing any animal into your family is a very important decision not to be made lightly. Once the decision has been made, everyone in the household must agree on a breed. No 3-2 or 3-1 or even 2-1. All have to agree because a dog is part of the family. Everyone in the family will be affected by and affect the behavior of the dog. There is NO perfect breed of dog because all have potential to be a positive member of the family. You all have to be aware that it will be work at first, especially with a young puppy.

You can read all you want about a breed and think that one sounds right. Understand that most of what you find will be breed characteristics of the breed standard. Breed standards are only a list of characteristics and visual description of the perfect representations for that breed. Yes, some of the characteristics are important, but a lot of dogs without proper teaching can have the same characteristics. Also, a lot of breeds have two types. The conformation show ring type and the field type. The difference in breeding types can make a big difference in drive (an innate, biologically determined urge to attain a goal or satisfy a need; genetic). Herding breeds drive to herd. Hunting breeds drive to smell, see, track, chase etc.. Understand that dog breeds originally were bred for a purpose/job. The urge to do a job is the dog's drive. You cannot teach out drive. You can only add fear to it. Fear-driven behavior is your fault not the dogs. They have not been allowed to do their job or at least something similar. High-drive dogs require brain and body exercise, if not supplied by the human. Dogs will find ways to exercise both, sometimes in a destructive manner.

I have lived with six different giant schnauzers (five females. one male). and I can honestly say they all were different even though structurally they all earned their championship in the conformation ring. South, the male, and Annie are the only two I helped raise from the litter. The other four were raised by others. Angel was 1 ½ years old and came from a very nice show farm. I can only guess she learned it was her job to catch and kill rabbits. Unaware of this, I was awakened one night to the sound of her vomiting and an awful smell. I got up to see and found raw rabbit flesh-ugh There is more to that story, but I will spare you. Faylyn grew up in a show family home with championship title. She was 4 years old and has not killed anything, but she finds it very important to keep her beard clean. None of the other four washed their beard in the water dishes like she does. Sometimes she also likes to dry it off on your pants leg while you are still in them. She weighs about 75 pounds, and either she doesn't realize her size or she is well aware of how big she is. If you are in a spot she likes to sleep in she has no problem jumping up and lying right on you. The newest girl sharing my life is Bailey. I recued her at 10 months of age from a family. First giant I ever saw lie down and eat with the bowl between her front legs. I could list other differences between them all but I think you get the point. Behaviors are not related to DNA but how and what they are taught is.

Ch Skansen's Miss Priss Mar-Vue

"Prissy"

Ch Ruster's What Dreams May Come
"Annie"

Ch Ruster's Southward Ho
"South"

Ch Ruster's Angel Band   Ch Skyline's Faraona ES Fabulosa
"Angel"   "Faylyn"

"Bailey"

Dominance

Alpha: denotes the dominant animal or human in a particular group.

Dominant: most important, powerful, or influential. (of a high place or object) overlooking others.

A pack is a group of animals/wolves/dogs just as a flock is of birds. Leader or boss of the pack, flock, herd, gaggle, pride, etc, is no different than a boss at work, a teacher in school, an Indian chief or a mother/father at home.

I cannot tell you how many times someone has said my dog is trying to be alpha or I have to show him/her I am alpha. I even see it on training sites. I have handled many dogs that had gone to a trainer who believes in that doo- doo. You can tell because the dog would fearfully submit or stand postured ready for a correction of some kind. Pack leader is a correct term according to the words humans have assigned for a specific animal/person and duty. The quarterback of a football team could also be called pack leader. Every group of humans or animals has to have someone step up to be the leader. Not all humans or animals choose to be leader but someone has to do it or there would be no order and nothing would get accomplished. Have you ever been in a job where there were too many chiefs and not enough Indians?

Dogs do not care to be in control, but if they are forced to care for themselves, they will for survival. It is up to the humans in the dog's life to be their teacher, coach, boss, chief, quarterback, mother/father, etc. When you decided to share your life with a dog, you agreed to be that for them. How the dog behaves in your family system is a reflection of how well you are providing everything you agreed to provide them. It is not just about food, water, and shelter. It is also about their understanding and well being. Dogs have two major states of being that are reflected in their behavior: love and fear. If you alpha them, you will only create deeper fear by validating the fearful behavior. Humans do not reinforce fear they reinforce the behavior the dog is exhibiting. The fear is there until the dog is taught differently. Address the fear, and the behavior changes. Alpha has nothing to do with it.

If you would like a dog to behave differently stop being alpha, no matter who you are-family member, groomer, vet tech, trainer, sitter, rescuer- any occupation that requires you to have your hands on a dog. A professional's job is not just to feed and water dogs, groom them, give them a shot, watch them when their humans are gone, etc. Our purpose, be it our job or our family, is to always defuse any fear. Love is the universal language in all species. Show love to defuse their fear.

"Alpha is force. Love is guidance."

Infant Humans-Infant Dog

Raising a puppy is not much different than raising a child. Both babies and puppies are cute, but the ways they are handled differ. With human infants, you tickle/kiss the soles of their feet, you caress/pinch/kiss their cheeks, you change a diaper even with kicking and screaming, you cut nails, the list goes on and on. Humans coddle puppies, carry them around everywhere and let them dictate what the human can do to them.

Human infants are born unable to walk. Totally dependent
Puppies are born deaf and blind. Totally dependent

Most infants can walk at 12-15 months. Have to watch or put in play pen. Out of diapers 18 months-4 years
Puppies can hear at three weeks and fully see at eight weeks. Have to watch or put in play pen. Potties outside consistently depends on age joined family and being taught.

Understanding what we are actually teaching can explain why the children/dogs may have fear. It is not about earning trust. Trust is a word humans created, and by definition is *a firm belief in the reliability, truth, ability, or strength of someone or something.* Trust is a learned behavior pattern associated to a specific action/reaction. If you constantly hit something in the face, that is what they will set as a pattern by everyone. Children and puppies will become hand shy to all humans until taught not all humans will hit them.

Human Infant

Tickling/kissing soles of feet-Touch of different types on the feet stimulates different emotional feelings. Warm lips/comforting, tickle/electrical energy transfer triggering an energy rush feeling in body. Even putting on socks is a new experience and different feeling physically and emotionally.

Caress/kissing/pinching cheeks-Like touching the feet, you are teaching different physical feelings, and you are learning infants' emotional behavior response for that action. You are aware that what you are doing is not hurting them physically, unless you pinch too hard. If you receive a negative response for an action, you talk calmly and show them you are not hurting them.

Diaper change-Besides the obvious reason, this is also a routine action response that can be associated with a wet, nasty feeling being removed. For the feeling to be removed, the action of holding legs by ankle and being lifted up must be done. This is a learned behavior pattern the adult human creates. If you gave in to the kicking when you hold the ankles, you would never get the diaper changed. Cleaning/wiping is a feeling they have to get used to. Kisses hugs when finished becomes an associated pattern they learn.

Nail cutting-A must so the parent has no choice but to find the easiest way to do this. How do they do that? By showing the child you are not going to hurt them and also letting them know it is something that has to be done for their health and safety. If they pull, you don't yell at them. You just hold whatever it is they are pulling until they stop. Once they see what you are doing, they learn they have nothing to fear.

Puppy/ Dog

Feet and hands = Four paws and they are maps of the body. Handling, tickling and such of a puppy's/dog's paws not only stimulates the whole body, it gets them used to different feelings on the paws. This is one where being small and cute can create issues. Small and cute are carried around for everything. Not only is this unhealthy for muscle tone, it can also cause the puppy to be unsure of standing on different table and floor surfaces.

Face caresses are a non-threatening way of showing it is OK "I love you," creating a calming, relaxed feeling. Human and canine alike at an older age is more accepting of having their face washed/wiped, eyes cleaned, and teeth checked if they had a lot of positive facial contact when young.

Diaper changing humans can be compared to brushing and cleaning up accidents in dogs. Brushing dogs at least once or twice a week is nothing compared to how many times you have to change a diaper or brush a child's hair. Humans say the dog will not let them do it. Was this the same for your children? Did you not brush their hair because they did not let you?

Nail cutting is the same, just a different type. Those of you who have your dog groomed at least every six weeks do not have to be concerned about nails. Puppies and some dogs have very sharp nails that can get caught on things, so it is important to cut them. They are going to struggle as much as a human baby and may even cry as a human baby would. The thing a puppy might do that a child won't is try to bite. Stay calm and show them it is no big deal. "But I am afraid of making them bleed." I keep a container of septic powder with my clippers so I can stop any bleeding I cause by cutting the kwik. No fear of cutting the hyponychium (informally known as the quick or kwik) because I can make it stop bleeding. Hold pressure on the toe before you cut nail to prevent blood rushing out if kwicked. It is more that sudden warm feeling that the dog is reacting to.

Rescue or Purchase from Breeder

The whole family has agreed to bring puppy/dog home, promising to love and care for them till the day their body shuts down. Now it's time to decide whether to adopt a rescue or purchase from a breeder.

In my first book "Behind the Doggy Door" (available on Amazon). I talk about some of my experiences in the different fields. In every field of dogs, humans are profiting and not caring for them like they deserve.

Severely injured or crippled rescue dogs being kept alive is only for the benefit of the humans involved. Advertising these dogs in any way gets other humans to feel sorry and donate to the cause. Has this dog not suffered enough? Quality of life-what does that mean to you? I talk about this in Chapter 3, "Dealing with Death."

Humans are the ones to blame for any dog needing rescue in the first place. At the shelter you see all kinds of things humans do to dogs. At first it was unbelievable, but after time it became common. The shelter I worked at did not adopt out injured or crippled dogs, not even to the rescue groups. I would love to see that in all shelters. There are plenty of healthy dogs brought into shelters that could be adopted.

Rescue vs. Purchase

Dogs at shelters/rescue groups are going to have fears. These fears will be reflected in their behavior. In Chapter 2, I give examples of different behavior types I have observed. These different types are taught by the humans in the dog's life.

Dogs live by patterns they have learned from experiences. These patterns take time to change. When adopting a rescue dog, you will be dealing with teaching different patterns of life in a loving manner. The age of the dog will tell you how long this dog has been living life in this fear pattern. I mentioned you can teach old dogs new patterns, but is that humane to the dog?

I have mentioned a dog is only aware of the life they live. Adopting or purchasing an older (7 and up depending on breed) dog from a puppy mill and expecting it to be the perfect family dog is rare. These dogs have spent their whole life having babies, every heat cycle, in unsanitary environments. Going potty where they stand, eat, sleep, and mother is all they know. Most are so unhealthy they are barely alive. Buying from a breeder these dogs will have been bred as many times as the breeder bred. Possibly raised on a farm, a kennel-learned behaviors connected to living.

It is not their fault. That is what they have been taught by the humans in their life. Puppies learn from their mothers, so the behavior patterns mom has will be learned. A puppy 7 months or younger has not spent years living with specific patterns. This age range is easily taught different behavior patterns with love and understanding. A puppy 7 months and older will depend on if they have been bred. They may or may not have some major fears from the experience. Having them spayed will reduce some fears. If they are possessive of specific toys, allow them to be. They will get over it in their time. It is only up to the human to teach that no fear is necessary.

Health issues

When adopting or purchasing, there is a chance the dog has health issues. Some health issues in a puppy can kill them. The conditions, the puppy was raised in will alert you to the possibility of a possibe deadly disease. Parvo and distemper are two of the top viral illnesses killing puppies from unethical breeders.

Unless the rescue group saw the conditions they were raised in, you have no idea what you are getting. Going to breeder you can see where and how they were raised. If a breeder does not allow you to see, walk away. Not only do you see the conditions, you also get to see the puppy's parents. If lucky, you can also see grandparents. A puppy will resemble them more as adult. Also, the other dogs' behavior around them will be learned by them.

Breed-specific Genetic Conditions

Different breeds carry different genes for specific medical conditions. How the breeder monitors their dog's and avoids it in breeding is key. Does the breeder care about the health of the puppies or the money? Breeding for a specific look and not caring about health is not uncommon. A reputable breeder will have health records and or certificates (OFA Cerf, and DNA (males) for all of the dogs they breed.) Paying more for this type of guarantee is not for everyone. Prices for dogs are outrageous to say the least. Designer dog breeds (mixes) are the ones that cost the most.

Here you have two different breeds with different and the same genetic conditions being mixed. You also get different drive levels and purposes combined in one dog. Some conditions in small breeds are not uncommon or deadly like luxating patellas and heart murmurs. If monitored by breeders, though, these health conditions could be eliminated from their breeding program.

Breeders who guarantee the health of a puppy care about what they are producing. I was one of those breeders for a few years. I had two golden retriever puppies returned by the same individual and gave them their money back. One had odd health issues. The other was not the first one behavior wise. As a breeder, I was responsible for what I produced no matter what.

It is not the breeders of any puppy who has their heart ripped out when something causes pain or kills the family puppy. I saw a few of these cases when I worked at the specialty clinic. Breeders in these cases were unavailable to the purchaser or the purchaser got "Oh, well."

When the family is thinking about bringing a dog into the family, make time to sit together and go over the breeds preferred, age, color, and sex.

Take the list and look up breed specific conditions for each breed. Now you are aware of what questions to ask and what to watch for. no matter where you decide to go…rescue or breeder.

Chapter Two
Bringing Home

"Lucy" "Roger" "Bouche"

The first few months of a puppy's life are important for development of behavior patterns. Puppies that leave the litter at six weeks cannot fully see, and their behavior will reflect that. All experiences they have thus far are by hearing, smelling, and feeling. Puppies that leave litter at eight weeks can see fully for the first time. All behavior patterns have been learned by hearing, smelling, and feeling. Puppies that stay with the litter until they are twelve weeks of age have learned to watch body language in association to smell, sound, and feeling.

Having a plastic enclosed kennel or playpen ready for your puppy when you bring it home helps comfort them and keep them safe. Letting a puppy loose in a large home can be overwhelming to them as well as dangerous. That would be like letting a child who can crawl unattended in a strange home. Keeping them confined with their toys and a bed will help them become more relaxed with all the new sounds, smells, and sights. Wire kennels make clanging noises when the dog walks on the pan. A dog that is already afraid may have a bad reaction. Wire kennels also need to be covered, only leaving the door area open. A fearful dog has to guard all sides. Vari Kennel has one way in one way out like a cave. It also does not have a clanky pan.

Kennels help teach puppies to go potty outside-just like putting a small child in a playpen teaches independence and self-entertainment. Be sure to give the puppy things that they are allowed to tear up. That way they will learn what is theirs so when you catch them chewing on something else, you can trade them mine-yours. Know that anything on the ground is fair game to a puppy until they learn.

So just like baby proofing, it is good to puppy proof before you even bring the puppy home. If you do not want it torn up, pick it up out of the puppy's reach. If there are things you cannot get out of their reach, keep a close eye on them when loose or block them from it. Always put the puppy up if you have to do something that prevents you from being able to watch them. Once a puppy/dog has gone potty or chewed something up out of your sight, they will do it again because they were not caught before doing so.

Relax

If you have ever watched a mother with her pups, you see how she rolls them over to clean them. The first few times this happens, the puppy struggles trying to turn back upright. After time, though, they learn they are not going to get hurt and roll over relaxed and let mom clean them.

Above I talked about some of the different things we have to do to children and puppies and how it stimulates them. Studies show that early neurological stimulation can benefit the dog in many ways. Doing actions to a puppy similar to mom's can help reduce the puppy's fear of the unknown. I have personally done this to every litter I've had. I especially made sure to do it every day on two single puppy litters. It is more important to do this with single-litter pups because they do not have littermates to compete with and constantly stimulate them by going over them or pushing them out of the way.

I had to hand raise one puppy because mom rejected it. This puppy was born with a cleft lip and had very large moleras (soft spots) on his skull. The other puppy was just a single-litter puppy that I felt needed it. The one I raised by hand was fed every two hours and then stimulated to go potty. With him, I would lay him on his back in my hand and lightly stimulate his whole body by lightly scratching it. I would also rotate him back and forth, front to back. Sometimes I would tickle his toes while he was on his back. I would rub his belly to get him to relax.

He was born with a very large molera in the center of his skull and multiple moleras. I would rub his head every chance I got to be sure he had good blood circulation. He developed well, but when he started to walk I noticed he was off. He seemed to be more comfortable walking backward than forward. I continued the regular stimulation and massaging his head. I then started putting him on the waterbed and got him to walk to me. The unsteadiness of the bed seemed to help him be surer of himself on a flat surface. In litters, puppies constantly have to climb over each other so they learn better footing. He, however, had nothing he had to climb over. Even his stuffed animal did not cause him to be unsure of his footing. He mainly climbed on it and went to sleep.

He grew to adulthood, very healthy with a small molera, which is normal. His cleft lip did not cause any problems. The only issue was that he did not care to be around other dogs. Since he was solely raised by human hands, he only knew humans. Over time he learned other dogs were all right.

With the early stimulation provided by mom and littermates in the first few weeks of life, a puppy will start to develop behavior patterns. Here again being with their littermates and mom helps them develop some acceptable behavior. A puppy's littermates and mom will correct them if they become too defensive, teaching them to be easier/calmer. Most of the times you will see mom hold the puppy down with her foot or muzzle, until it calms down. Both the littermates and the mom are teaching there is nothing to fear, calm down. What does a puppy have to fear you ask? When they were blind and deaf, they accidently got stepped on by mom or they got laid on by mom and could not breathe. They can hear and have some degree of sight and have teeth. Getting bitten by littermates now comes into play. Would that not cause you to have some fear?

Another thing puppies learn from their litter is survival of the fittest. When it is time to wean the puppies off mom, most breeders feed in a litter pan. This means all the puppies eat together or they miss out on a meal. Having this type of competition teaches the puppy to eat all of his/her food when fed and prevent picky eaters. The ways humans control any behavior situations determines if a puppy learned to protect their food.

Puppies that are removed from the litters between 6-8 weeks have experienced life with being able to fully see. That is why they bite or growl when you do something to them. A puppy learns from its littermates the acceptable or unacceptable pressure of a play bite. If they bite hard on a fearful puppy, it will scream and run away. If they bite too hard on a defensive, high drive puppy, it will turn around and bite the fire out of them. If they bite hard on mom, she will growl and probably snap at them. All the different responses teach them the proper bite/mouthing behavior.

If they are not defensive you may have one that is scared of everything it encounters. The slightest movement scares them or loud sound scares them. Some puppies may fear the unknown because their known has not been all positive. How much human interaction are they patterned to? A confident well handled puppy has no fear.

If you must get a puppy before 12 weeks of age, it is important not to coddle them. I have always patted my puppies behind, like a spanking, in fun saying, "Beat your butt". As they got older when I did this they would get excited and run around then come back for more. One day I was holding a friend's puppy and I did this to get it happy. The puppy screamed bloody mercy as if I was beating it. It surprised me let alone the puppy. I told the human they needed to stop babying the puppy and get it used to being handled. Most of the puppies I have spoken about so far are chihuahua puppies. Yes, they are cute and cuddly, but they are not china dolls. No need to treat them that way.

Puppies of all ages can benefit from external stimuli also. They do not need to be carried all over, but if they are going to be around a lot of humans they need to be handled by more than one human. These puppies are too young to be socialized due to lack of vaccinations. Humans who come to visit, however, can handle them for short periods of time. The neurological stimulation is still good for all ages. It is good to have everyone in the family do some of these stimulation exercises regularly.

Putting the puppy on its back on the couch and rubbing its belly is good. If they are struggling, just hold them, still talking to them calmly until they relax. Then let them up and praise them, teaching them you are not going to hurt them. Continue this daily until they lay calm and let you rub their tummy. You can also do the same by laying them between your legs instead of the couch. Once they have become comfortable lying on their back, start rubbing their feet. This teaches them that you are not going to hurt them. Using different textures on their feet will help them be less sensitive to rocks, cold, or other things they may walk on. This will also help when you need to cut their nails or do anything to their feet. So many dogs hate you to just touch their foot. Starting to mess with them young helps the dog learn they have nothing to fear when they are older.

As a groomer, I could tell the puppies that had been coddled from the ones that have been socialized and handled a lot. Some clients even told me they got out a blow dryer and just blew it on their puppy to get them used to it. That is good because if you do have to bathe a puppy at a young age, you must dry them completely so they do not get a chill. Be aware that a puppy will cry out or try to bite if they are fearful. You know what you are doing is not hurting them so do not let them, go or they learn it. This is very important because humans create the behavior patterns that the dog lives by and is prepared for.

Think about how you would handle giving a baby a bath. The first few times they may be afraid and cry. You know you are not hurting them so staying calm and talking in a soft voice will relax them and they will see they are fine. If a child told you "no," would you listen to them? Then why let a puppy tell you no?

Rest

Puppies are wild learning machines that require rest. Scheduled nap time is important for very young puppies. Young puppies can have hypoglycemic episodes if they do not rest. This happens because they are so busy running around and playing that they burn all the sugar they received at their mealtime. This can cause the puppy to faint and even go into a coma until the sugar level is brought up in their system.

Having a closed-in space for a puppy to sleep in will help them feel more secure. An enclosed kennel or a human playpen works great. I put stuffed animals along with a portable clock or loud watch under them to simulate a heart beat so they feel less alone. It is also helps them feel less alone if you put a family members dirty shirt from the day. Placing over stuffed animals with clock under to them is like sleeping on the human's chest.

Taking a puppy away from its litter before it is at least 11-12 weeks can be very traumatic to them. Letting them sleep with you is not a great idea. They have to learn to be independent and gain their own kind of security. Enclosed kennels or playpens are great for puppies to stay safe in and teach them they have nothing to fear. We have domesticated them enough. We do not want to make them so dependent on us and fear being alone. Teaching them to be independent helps them gain confidence in themselves. Is this not what parents do with human babies? A lot of these worries can be avoided if you do not take a puppy home before it is at least 12 weeks old.

Another reason it is good to not get a puppy younger than 12 weeks is because of shots. A puppy's first vaccination is usually given at six weeks of age. The second at nine weeks, third at 12 weeks, and the fourth/last at 15-16 weeks of age.

Some breeders give their own vaccinations. This is good because the puppies do not have to go to a strange place and get poked by a strange human with a sharp object alone. If the breeder does use a vet, at least the puppy will be with their littermates to bring them comfort and security. You do not want a puppy's first experience at a clinic to be a traumatic one. So if they had two sets of vaccinations with the littermates, that third and fourth one will be a piece of cake to them. The only thing they have to be concerned about is the strange person poking and prodding them. Having strangers do something to them in a professional capacity is something that they will have to learn to get used to. Different places and different humans are great experiences for the confidence building a puppy needs to mature into a sound, fearless adult.

A responsible breeder will not let a puppy leave before it is 12 weeks old.

Once a puppy has had at least three sets of shots, they can start being socialized. To teach a puppy not to fear strange humans, expose them to plenty of people. Have them hold and play with the puppy. Understand though you can over humanize a dog. I groomed plenty of puppies that feared the other dogs in the room. That is because they had not been socialized with other dogs, just humans.

This can also work the other way. Puppies/dogs that have only been around dogs fear humans. These puppies/dogs can become fear biters or wet themselves when a human approaches. A puppy/dog that has never been exposed to loud noises, lots of humans, other dogs or fighting humans has no clue how to respond to it. You have to expose your puppy to as much as you can so they will not fear the unknown. Dropping pans gets them used to loud sounds as long as the human does not feel bad for scaring them. When Bailey first moved in, I would hide places in the house to scare her. One time I jumped out from behind the counter in the kitchen and she jumped sideways so dramatically and barked. I started laughing and once she realized it was me, she ran over to me all wiggly.

Puppies/Dogs Learned Patterns

We are always teaching our puppies/dogs new patterns of life. Some of these patterns humans set they are not aware they are teaching or the possible long-term effect. When teaching, sometimes humans create patterns that can be somewhat confusing to dogs. Then there are others that learn really quickly but it is not the pattern trying to be taught.

The best example of this is teaching the puppy to potty outside. It does not matter if it is a puppy or older dog, they learn the pattern. I have had many clients ask how to stop their dog from going potty in the house right after they come in from outside. The first question I ask is what do you normally do as soon as the dog comes in from being outside? Everyone has a morning and night routine that any animal becomes a part of. One played with the dog as soon as it came in. Another gave treats at the door as they came in. Do you see the pattern?

Anything a dog finds to be fun, fantastic, wonderful, and tasty/ rewarding in anyway, trumps going potty outside. Sound familiar? Tasty treats are one thing a dog loves, and most will do anything to receive them. This, however, sets a pattern to them that if they do this, they get goody. A dog taught with goody rewards mixes up English words because they are too focused on getting that goody. I have seen dogs taught with treats anticipate what word will be spoken and do all of the actions they learned associated to treats. All they are aware of at that moment is that goody they can already taste.

To stop a behavior you cannot live with, you change the pattern. A dog that continues to have accidents when it comes in from outside, can be put in a kennel, play pen, or room. Any- where. It is no big deal if they have an accident. Feed them and take them back outside 10-20 minutes later. A dog that is having accidents will continue to do so unless you change your pattern.

Remember you set the time for the dog/s to get up in the morning, even puppies. A very young puppy will have accidents in their beds because they cannot hold it. Hold time capability increases with age like a human child. Handle all types of situations is something you signed up to for when the dog joined the family. Cleaning up after puppy is a big job depending on the age. A puppy is not crying because it needs to go potty, it is crying because it is lonely. Sure, if you take it out at 3a.m. it probably will go-however that is not what you are teaching them. You are teaching cry=get out of enclosure.

These are just a couple of examples. The point is to look at what pattern the behavior is attached to and change the pattern instead of getting angry at the dog.

"Beans"

Attention Span

Between 4 months and 6 months, a puppy's attention span is very short. They will only pay attention to you for about 15 minutes at a time. Once that time is up, they are off in another world looking for what they can play with or chew up.

It is good to start working with a puppy on little tasks like sit. Remember though they will only pay attention to you for about 15 minutes. As soon as they understand word action association, praise and love on them and then go play or take them out to play.

Puppies

In life there is no right or wrong way to do things. There are however, ways to do something that will create a positive or negative response. Each puppy can have a different response for each person involved in its life.

Puppies do not understand human words until they have been shown the action association. Over and over I see humans yelling "come" to a puppy. The puppy has no clue what they are asking of them. Most women usually start out soft voiced, increasing volume each time they have to repeat. That gets no response, so they might try and catch the puppy. At first the puppy is confused so may come and then run away. After time, the puppy learns this chasing game is fun until the human gets tired and angry. Now it avoids humans at all costs. Some men expect the puppy to know exactly what they are saying, so they are angry right away when the chasing begins. That puppy feels that anger and only wants to get away from it.

Put yourself in the puppy's position. Someone is yelling at you in a foreign language. You have no clue what they are saying as they head toward you with something in their hand. What do you do? Are you going to go running to them or away from them? If you do go to them and they really fuss at you or even hit you when you get to them will you do that again?

Do not chase a puppy/dog that is running from you. Squat down, run the opposite direction, hide behind a tree, laugh, and make all kinds of happy noises that they enjoy being around. You have no right getting angry at them because you have not taught them by showing them the association with the word to an action. You instead are showing them that when you say "come" they are to run so you can chase them or they are going to get fussed at if they come to you. It is not wise to call anyone or anything to you so you can then discipline. If someone called you to come over and they slap you in the face. Would you go the next time they called you over? You may not be saying it out loud, but it is a pattern you are setting with your puppy.

Until you have worked together with your puppy, even adopted older dogs, it is best to walk them on lead so they can begin to understand word action association, even in a fenced yard.

Also do not give treats for anything they do. This can cause a bad pattern that will be harder to break than to not start at all. Praise, toys and hugs work better than treats because of the physical energy exchange. Change of reward will not set them in a specific reward per action. They learn some kind of great reward when they listen.

The best way to prevent bad patterns from forming is to set good ones from the start. An example would be to take the puppy out first thing in the morning when you get up. Bring them in and let them free keeping an eye on them. Do not play with them or give them a lot of attention or you may kennel them back up for 5-10 minutes. If kenneled, feed them. If free, kennel and feed. Fifteen-20 minutes after they eat, take them outside again so they can go potty. Most puppies will not poop first thing in the morning. They will, however, need to poop 10-20 minutes after they eat. Every time you leave or go to bed, take them outside before putting them in their kennel. Take outside as soon as you wake up or get home. This way they will learn a routine and know what is expected and learn they are to go potty outside.

Be sure to set up a daily routine that you will be able to continue for the first few months of the puppy's life in the family. They pick up on routines really quickly and changing it on them can cause them to get confused, creating destructive behavior. Once they get older, then the routine can very a bit without confusing them. They may have behavior changes, but they will adapt quickly.

"Minnie"

Puppies will chew on things unless taught differently. Starting around 4 months of age, they will chew on stuff because they are teething. You can not scold them for chewing up things. They will not understand what they have done unless you catch them and stop them in the act. The only way to prevent them from chewing on everything and anything during this time is to supply them with plenty of things they can chew on. When a human baby is teething, parents normally give them teething rings and such to chew on. This gives them something good to chew on instead of their blankets, play pen rails, their shoes, etc.

They make plenty of chew toys to help with teething. Rawhide chews are okay if they are not bleached and/or have knots on each end. I have had two dogs choke on a knot they swallowed. The rawhide sticks are the best. Even if they swallow a large piece of one, it will go down and softened up in the stomach. **You do have to keep an eye on them when they have them**. One time I gave a golden retriever puppy, "Pheonix," a long chew stick. I was shocked to walk in a few minutes later and it was gone. Looking around I could not find it anywhere. She was sleeping so I looked at her and noticed a lump on her side. I ran my hand across her side, and lo and behold there was the chew stick. She had swallowed the whole thing. I knew it would not kill her, but she did need to relax until the acids in her stomach softened it up. A few hours later she was fine with no lump. From that point on, when I bought those long chew sticks, I cut them in half for her.

You must give puppies plenty of things they are allowed to chew up. We had to throw away three kitchen chairs because the same golden retriever puppy used the legs as a chew sticks. I could not get mad at her because I did not supply her with plenty to chew on. That was my fault, not hers. That is why I am aware that humans cause a lot of behavior issues our puppies have. These months are so important on setting patterns and also admitting what we did wrong when the puppy does something wrong.

What do you do when one day you go into your room and find one of your favorite shoes torn to shreds? Of course you get mad, but who are you mad at? The puppy at this point does not even remember going in there and tearing it up. So if you fuss at it, it will have no idea what you are fussing about, even if you show it the shoe. This is one of those cases where you only have yourself to blame or the family member who allowed the puppy to roam freely with-out supervision.

The same is true if you find an accident somewhere in your home. If you are not monitoring the puppy at all times, you can not reprimand the puppy for something you did not see it do. Now if you are watching and you see they are about to potty in the house, calmly pick them up or put on a lead and take them outside. saying "potty outside" (or what you choose). You are teaching them what "potty outside" means so they can understand and not be afraid. If you see them going toward or already chewing on something they are not supposed to chew on, give them something that is theirs and tell them "mine, this is yours" and give it to them.

From 7 months of age on, a puppy's attention span increases. They will learn all the patterns of humans in the family. Each human in the home has different patterns of action reactions. It is these patterns that set the stage for being part of the family. A puppy that is raised with anger/fear will attempt to bite when they feel threatened or confused. They will try everything they can think of to get you to stop doing anything they are fearful of.

When my mom brushed my hair, I would fuss trying to get her to stop. Of course, that did not work. Some children throw fits when they do not want to do something. Puppies might exhibit similar behavior out of fear of the unknown. If you would not let a child get away with this type of action, why would you let a puppy? I have heard so many humans say the puppy would not let them. Score one for the puppy. It has just learned and taught the pattern of how to get the human to stop. That is the same with a child. Here again, how can these other books say not to treat a puppy/dog like it is human. We took them from their canine families and brought them into our human families, so it is up to us to teach them how to live our lives.

I have adopted dogs in this age range. One giant was 8 months old and had been raised mainly in a chain link run with a concrete floor. Spending most of her time in the run, she learned it was OK to potty where she was, so she did not understand why it was not OK to just stop and urinate in the living room. Though it scared her, the first few times she was caught and taken outside. It did not take her long to learn that that behavior was not acceptable in her new home.

Ch. Skansen's Miss Priss Mar-Vue
"Prissy"

A puppy/dog learns different patterns of responses that I call types. Understanding these types will help you teach a different behavior response. Some dogs can be more then one type due to different situations in their life. It is just like multiple children in a family. Each child falls into the pattern response they learned. You have the troublemaker always needing attention. You have the clown, always needing the laugh to lighten the mood in the home. You have the quiet one who just stays out of it all, to name a few.

Seven-ten months is the most common age range that humans send a puppy to be taught obedience by someone else. Obedience-trained dogs are dogs competing for titles. The average human family does not require an obedience-trained dog. From the time the family takes in a dog, they have been teaching them. An outside teacher will address the behavior but not always address the reason for the behavior. The dog learned it somewhere, and even if they do change the behavior it does not guarantee the dog will not go back to old patterns once home. It is the family patterns, and if they stay the same the dog has no choice but to resort back no matter what they learned elsewhere.

A dog's behavior is their learned patterns of dealing with different situations. This is how they have learned or have been taught to behave in different situations. I have my own terms for each type of behavior. Others may have different ones. No matter what term you use, understanding how your dog will respond is the key to having a happy family system. No matter the type they are now, be aware that they can change with proper handling. Being aware of their type does not mean to feel for them. If you feel sorry or angry, they will learn that feeling. That feeling along with the human's action will become a pattern. I laugh at them for their specific behavior response. Laughter feels good to us, and it is an energy dog's love.

Understanding why a dog behaves a specific way and how they learned that behavior is the key at any age.

The table below has the type (in human terms) on top and how the dog might have learned a specific behavior response below.

Type I – Soft Dog This type takes everything very personally. They cower if you yell at them. They also may run and hide if there is any yelling even if it is not directed at them. Once you have identified them as being soft, it is easier to teach them new patterns. You never want a dog to do something out of fear. With soft dogs this is very important because if they do things out of fear, they can also pick up behavior patterns like fear biting or fear urination. Staying calm and talking softly when working with them helps build their confidence so they are not so sensitive. Praising them and loving on them also helps build their confidence and understanding. For every good thing they do, praise and reward them. Rewards can be anything from petting, giving them their favorite toy, to anything they really enjoy and get excited over.

Learned Behavior

There might be a puppy in the litter that was stepped on and laid on by accident by mom and picked on by littermates and afraid of almost everything.

Unlike more defensive responses, soft dogs are doing their best to understand what is happening. If these dogs were human, they would be apologizing all the time for nothing. If you were to give this type a collar correction, they would become very submissive, cowering and possibly urinating on self. A soft dog was raised in a home with a lot of arguing between humans that sometimes got physical. Dogs in these types of homes do not know if they are also being yelled at. They hide until everything calms down and avoid getting involved. A lot of soft dogs are also happy fear pacifiers.

"Phoenix"

Type II – Goosey Lucy This type reacts to touch like you have cooties. No matter where you try to touch them, they cringe just seeing your hand near them. Some are so sensitive to touch they will even jump sideways when you attempt to pet them. This can be hard when you want to love on them or give them a loving pat for doing something good. By working with them when they are young, you can show them that they do not have to fear touch. When I come across a goosey dog, I make sure to pet them all over and show them I am not going to hurt them. I also pat them down talking softly and even laughing so they see all is OK and feel the good energy rush over them. For ones that are overly goosey, I will goose them and make it into a game. As long as you never get mad at them for being that way, they will get over it if you touch them every chance you get.

Learned Behavior

A puppy in a litter that was not handled much by humans, a puppy born at a puppy mill or from a single-puppy litter, might not be familiar with human touch. Hand shy and goosey Lucy are different in that it is not the hand they fear, just the touch. A hand shy puppy has been smacked a lot. Tess was a single puppy in her litter. She joined the family at 11 weeks of age. Ivy and Secret, also LC chihuahuas were five days younger so Tess joined them in the human play pen.

Ch Kandee's Simply Pawfect "Tess"

Type III – Chicken Dog This type cracks me up because they spook at some of the funniest things. Imagine a beefy bull mastiff spooking at a wind chime and seeing a large dog like that stretching out so much that his stomach is almost touching the ground just to creep up on the chime. I could not help but burst out laughing and called him a chicken dog. He turned around, wagged his tail, and looked at me like "What, it scared me, what is it?" The best way to handle a chicken dog is to always allow them to approach what it is that they are scared of. Play spook them as they get closer and laugh. You can also take whatever it is and put it on the ground and give them time to approach it. In some cases, it is good to take whatever spooked them and pet the dog with it. I once had a dog that was a chicken dog when it came to plastic grocery bags. So every time I got home from the grocery store, I would empty the bags and throw them on the floor. Once the dog approached it on their own, I picked them up and touch their side with it. Eventually I was able to pet the dog with the plastic bag and they no longer were afraid of it. As long as you do not force anything or get angry with them, they will get over being a chicken dog.

Learned Behavior

There might be a puppy in a litter that was not exposed to different sounds, objects, and places. They can also be from a single-puppy litter.

This applies in a human family except the puppy might not be exposed to different sounds related to angry humans. Those sound patterns are learned.

"Ch Stonehill's Jade Mist" Jay"

"Jay" LC Chihuahua joined the family from a show breeding kennel. I showed her and she was afraid of the show camera man and the thing he threw. She was so afraid I started just holding her for pictures. To add to her fear of standing on a table at a show once I stacked her on the table for the judge to examine and a large table fell in the building, making a very loud echoing bang. It took time to show her I would not let her get hurt.

Type IV – Happy Fear Pacifier This type is not sure if it should fear something or be interested in it. I call them Happy Fear Pacifier because they will get scared and grab a toy and still bark with it in their mouth. They are not getting the toy to protect them, they just need that little bit of security. This type needs a lot of outside exposure. They are really good with other dogs and humans. They just fear the newness at the time. Once they have approached the other dog or human, they drop the toy. Some may even try to get the other dog or human to play with the toy. This type has to have that pacifier toy to carry around when they are fearful or very excited. This type has low self - confidence, so getting them out and exposing them to different noises, different humans, and dogs will help them become more confident in themselves. Playing with a flirt pole and praising and "whoo hooing" when

36

they catch the toy and such will also help.

Learned Behavior

I have not seen one of these come straight from a litter. However, I am sure it could be possible.

In a human family this type has been raised with a lot of arguing and some physical conflict between humans. I know this type very well because I had two at the same time. Both were around 12 weeks or older when brought home. A that time I had a partner who was very insecure and used alcohol to avoid resolving their feelings.

Another way a puppy might learn this behavior is not being sure whether you will play with it or not. Picture this. Puppy is playing out in the yard, and human calls them to come. They have not learned this word, but they love their human so they go running to them. They get close, and the human repeats in a different tone out of frustration or anger. What do you do next? From that point on they will be cautious when called and have the toy for security to see if human does want to play.

"Hope"

Type V – Drama Queen This type acts like everything you do to them is killing them. With this type it is best to teach them in the privacy of your home or yard. If other humans are around who feel sorry for them, this type might double the over-reaction. This type has learned body language associated to a specific action reaction. If a specific learned negative movement is made by the human, they are quick to react.

When teaching, do everything slowly and give them time to do as asked. Pet and pat them every chance you get. Teach them they no longer have to live in that pattern and that you will never hurt them. Do not feel sorry for them. This will only make them more reactive because they feel that energy from you. When playing it is good to play a little rough but not over-powering with this type. Build their confidence.

Bailey still behaves like this type when she has a little fear. When she first got here, she would over-react when I asked her to do something and I went toward her to show her. She would jump crazily sideways when I would step toward her like I was about to tackle her. She slammed her body down when asked to lie down, like if not the human would. Just to name a few.

Learned Behavior

There might be a puppy in the litter that learned this crazy behavior scared off the other puppies. A human will put down in fear.

In a human family this type was raised with a lot of negative physical reactions from the humans. Hitting, jerking, pushing, throwing things at them, forced, etc

Bailey joined the family at 10 months of age from a family. More details after table.

"Bailey"

Type VI – Happy Pleaser This may sound like a great dog. However, this dog wants to please so badly it does the wrong thing because it anticipates what you are going to say. Soft dogs are pleasers exhibiting submissive behavior. A happy pleaser exhibits more hyper behavior. They can be so gung-ho that they actually have the wiggles trying to do what you ask before you finish asking them. The best way to handle this type is to just stay calm and get them to calm down so they can pay attention. Sometimes it is best to wear this dog out a bit before you try to teach them anything. I have known a few dogs like this.

Two of them were golden retrievers. Another was a field bred springer spaniel. The only way I could get them to calm down enough to listen was to wear them out first by playing ball. Now I swear by flirt poles, homemade or purchased. Once they played a little, working their brain and body, they were attentive to me. All were very high-drive dogs, so releasing some of the built-up energy was the only way to get them calm enough to listen to what was being asked. As they get older, their drive energy does decreases. However, you do have to exercise brain and body on a regular basis or dog will get stuck in destructive patterns. Staying calm is also key. It can take up to five years in some breeds for their drive to decrease.

Learned Behavior

There might be a puppy in the litter raised with very active dogs, trying to keep up with the gang not to miss out on brain and body work.

This type is more often found in field breeds bred specifically to work the field. They were bred to hunt, herd, protect, etc. That is the drive different breeds are bred for and when not released, that energy will build. Not only do they have that energy building, they also have fear energy because the human is frustrated or angry. They do things fast so as not to get a correction because they have not learned word-action association. They have been too excited, unable to focus on what the human is doing and saying.

Dogs taught with treats can also be a happy pleaser. They are so focused on the treat, they don't hear what you say. They go through every action related to

that goody.   "Buddy" SAR Land

Type VII-Slow Poke McGraw. This type understands word action association. However, they do them slowly. There is not much you can do but give this type time. If you try to force them to be faster, some will go that much slower or even stand their ground and not move. It can get aggravating waiting for them to follow through, but they do get faster in time. The best thing to do with this type is to try and get them excited and happy about doing something. If you can get them excited and happy, it will reduce any fears they may have and they get faster to get your happy, feel-good praise.

*Note a dog in pain might exhibit this behavior. Always rule out a medical conditions first if it is a new behavior.

Learned Behavior

There might be a puppy in the litter that behaved over excited and constantly getting bullied or reprimanded by mom. A high-drive puppy is prevented from playing/pouncing on littermates. It sits in corner and is still and watches-very unsure of it all.

In the family they learned the human is going to handle them roughly. "Mason," 1 ½ years old, came to me from a rescue group labeled with aggressive behavior. He definitely behaved defensive of everything. He had been sent to an obedience training kennel for six weeks prior. Needless to say, "Mason" had been living his life in pure fear.

"Mason"

Type VIII-Distracted This type is more interested in seeing the sights than anything the human has to show them. To them chasing birds, squirrels, or anything else is more important.

This type differs from the happy pleaser because they are not even listening. They are constantly looking off and shutting out whatever it is you are asking of them. If you have ever taken your dog by the muzzle and turned their head to look at you, though they are facing you, and their eyes look to the side or elsewhere, then your dog is this type.

Brain games like the flirt pole are good as well as praising them every time they make eye contact. Teaching "leave it" will also help them take their attention off something else. You can also teach "watch me" by slowly turning their head, by their muzzle, toward your eyes. Do not force if they pull against you. Turn to where you are looking in their eyes blocking them from looking elsewhere repeating "leave it or watch me." Whatever term you choose, just be sure to use the same every time you want their attention. Teaching a dog with both verbal and hand signals can help keep the dog's attention on you. Sticking your tongue out and giving them a raspberry or making funny noises with your mouth can help get their attention. Once they make eye contact kiss them on the nose. They will want more loving, fun energy.

Learned Behavior

There might be a puppy in the litter that was raised in a happy litter environment. They are in awe of all the cool stuff around them.

A family dog has been asked to do something and if not done forced to do it. Another time, the dog is asked to something, and if not done, nothing happens. The dog has no consistency, so they have no pattern to follow. The distractions, however, have patterns that the dog loves being a part of.

"Bailey"

Type IX-Hard Dog This one is the polar opposite of the soft dog. They are the ones that act like they feel nothing. These are the ones that have it in their mind that you are not going to make them do anything. This type can also show defensive behavior when asked to do something. They have learned to fear the human's reaction.

The worst thing you can do with this type is to get angry with them. The best way to handle it is to act like their actions are not affecting you in any way. There are ways of being firm without being forceful. You may have to stand in front of or over them for a few to more minutes for them to finally sit. The more you touch them to get them to sit the more that pattern is what they learn. Waiting and repeating verbal once and hand signals as needed, will teach them you will not touch them but you will not move until they do as asked.

Learned Behavior

There might be a puppy in the litter that was stepped on, pushed around and laid on to the point it became a pattern so they learned to just deal with it.

The family dog has been physically corrected for specific behaviors. They learn to just get prepared for what's about to come and or to see if you mean what you are saying.

This type has learned everything about the human all the way down to heart rate associated to behavior response. If you become frustrated when teaching them, ask them to do something easy, praise like mad, then go to something else.

*A dog with thyroid issues could behave in a similar manner. Rule out first if new behavior.

Ch Ruster's Southward Ho "South"

Type X-Fear Defensive This type is afraid and might cry and growl simultaneously. I took in a SC Chihuahua ,"Lilly," who started biting children. One night I walked past her in her playpen. I heard her growl and cry, so I walked over to see what she was upset about. I noticed she had had an accident. I got a tissue and picked it up. I also picked up the blanket she had drug out of her bed. Once I moved it, I notice poop under it. She had tried to hide it so she did not get in trouble. I calmly told her it was OK, no biggy and cleaned it up. I fixed her bed back up and petted her softly. After a short time, she no longer feared getting in trouble for having an accident and the accidents stopped all together. You have to stay very calm with this type. They have had to defend themselves by trying to bite the human. Only if you catch them about to do something do you say anything.

"Lily"

Learned Behavior

There might be a puppy in the litter that learned this behavior got other puppies to leave them alone and not hurt them. There was little to no human interaction/intervention.

The family dog has received verbal and physical reprimands way after the act. They learn they get reprimanded for everything they do. Behavior response will come from fear. Small dog learns submissive urination or snapping defense gets a different reaction. Large dogs learn deep growling or snapping defense gets a different reaction. If you show any type of action out of anger you are validating their pattern of fearful behavior response as well as possibly creating more.

"Pete" 1 ½ year Jack mix would roll over and urinate. Being a male it would go up and back onto him. He was raised in a home with three 20 + guys. Then he was moved to a home with other 20 + guys and gals. "Pete" like all the others was behaving in fear.

"Pete"

Type XI-If I Must This type will do everything you ask of them perfectly but are like a robot. They go through the motions without any feeling. I lived with a Chihuahua "Billy" that was one of the easiest dogs I have ever had for teaching agility. He would go on any obstacle without fear, but he was lacking enthusiasm. No matter how happy I got with him, he was just ready to be done with these trivial exercises. The best way to handle this type is to find something else they really love doing. Not all dogs care to do what we have planned for them to do and forcing them will only

"Billy"

cause you and them unnecessary frustration.

Learned Behavior

This type just does not have any desire to do something dog related. I lived with a Jack "Tink" I rescued at five-six weeks of age from shelter found in watery ditch. She loved life but could care less about searching for humans. A golden retriever from a litter I helped raise "Aurie" preferred being on the couch to going out to the field to search for a human.

"Tink"

I will admit I spoiled both of them so I created this pattern. They both preferred being loved on and played with by me and a friend. The friend lived the next street over and came to visit a lot. "Tink" would search for her or me but no one else.

"Aurie" was the only one out of the litter that did not have the drive to search.

"Aurie"

Bailey came to me with other types besides the drama queen. She showed behavior responses from almost all types. Let me show you what this puppy went through from the time the family took her in until the time she came to me.

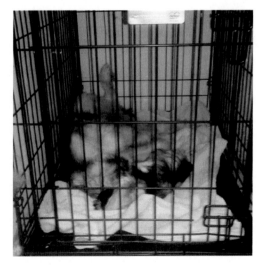

Bailey was raised in a family with two young children, one in a wheel-chair and two smaller dogs. I am not aware what happened prior to her getting her first grooming. I am aware that each time she came back, she behaved more fearfully.

The first time Bailey came to my friend's shop to be groomed, she was a typical 5 month-old puppy, but as you can see, she was able to relax.

Sept. 10, 2016 (photo)… 5 months old calm and relaxed

Nov. 27 Thanksgiving 7 ½ months old-imagine what she learned

Dec. 25 Christmas 9 ½ months old-imagine what she learned

Dec. 31 New Year's Eve fireworks

Feb. 27 Defensive behavior-vet recommended euthanasia

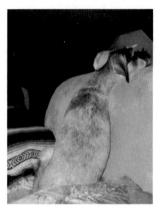

Bailey is the perfect example of nature vs. nurture behavior responses.

When she arrived at my home, her behavior was of total fear. She paced, not sure how to behave and in fear of doing something she might get yelled at for. She would sit with her back to the human.

Some dogs at this age will exhibit more defensive behavior when asked to do something out of fear. If they have not been shown it will not hurt them, they will continue to fear it. If you get defensive or show anger back, they will only get more defensive. I worked with a great Dane puppy that showed really bad defensive behavior. When the owners came to visit and see how he was doing, he showed his teeth toward me when leading him toward them. I just ignored it. However, I noticed the daughter laughing. I told her not to laugh at this type of behavior because it encouraged it to continue.

So no matter how cute it may be when a puppy is doing something wrong, never let them see you laughing at them. If they see you laughing, they think what they are doing is OK. So unless you are playing with them and they are being cute in an appropriate manner do not let them see you laugh. Some inappropriate behavior is best handled by ignoring it. It is no fun for them to not get any response to their actions. Others may require an appropriate response to the action. In my previous book "Understanding Behavior" I explain

Happy TAIL

Teach

Avoid

Ignore

Love.

I have heard and seen dogs do something they are not supposed to do and watched to see what the human is going to do. I worked with a lab that tore up plants and would run around with sticks in his mouth. It was not until his humans came to visit that I found out he did this at home and they would chase him to get the sticks. I also found out their son had played with him with a potted plant, when he was younger, to get him to chew it up.

The next time he did it to me. I grabbed another stick and took off running. He was so confused and surprised. I had to laugh. He was not sure what was going on. He came running after me and dropped the stick he had when I threw the one I had. I explained to his human family he loved this pattern. It was fun till it wasn't. He got a response, and he got humans to chase him. I explained how I handled it and also taught him "leave it." I broke the pattern and taught him something new.

I have seen many dogs at this age actually throw what a human would call a temper tantrum when they have to do something they are not sure of or are fearful. A dog, however, does not lie on the floor and scream and kick their feet during a fit. They more than likely will tear up something with a fierce frustration, this includes their own toys. Imagine how you feel when you are frustrated because you fear or do not understand something?

Dogs do not know English, but they can learn anything with repetition and consistency. Also 7 months of age and up they are more capable of learning the human tone of voice and the energy given off at any given time. The dog will learn the human emotional energy associated with the human's reactive patterned behavior.

The more frustrated or agitated you get, the more confused and agitated the gets. Dogs feel the energy you emit, and they will either fear it or become agitated because they do not know what to do. This is the same between dogs. If you have one dog that fears thunder, another dog in the home will feel this and sometimes do the same. Because dogs are so sensitive to feelings they are quick to pick up on and learn from them. During this age period, puppies are clean slates. They not only learn from their human family, they learn by example from other dogs in the home. How another dog responds to your emotions, the puppy will pick up on it.

"Bailey"

By the time the puppy is 18 months old, they can start to learn agility, search &rescue, or anything else that requires jumping or climbing. Since a dog is full grown at 18 months, you will not have to worry about joint injuries due to immature bones and ligaments. There are many organizations that go to shelters and adopt older dogs that are perfect for service dogs. They test the dogs to see which ones have the drive and which ones do not. If you are looking for a dog for some type of service dog, look for the high drive dogs.

You must give a high drive dog plenty of exercise and interaction. They have to have something to do to use up their physical and mental energy. That is why they are the best dogs for service work. They have a job that pleases the human. Though you may think specific breeds are better for different jobs, it is actually different dogs not the breed. Most would think all golden retrievers are great for service work. This is only true if they are specifically bred for drive. You cannot get a dog from two conformation champions and expect it to do service work. This only works if the dogs also had obedience titles. Dogs that are bred for the show ring are bred specifically for body structure and breed standard. Dogs bred for obedience or agility are bred for their drive to work.

By now the human's patterns of behavior have been learned by the dog. Humans might think they are testing them by not doing as asked. Things like, what I call selective hearing is the pattern they learned from the human saying something then walking away without following through. To them the human is just blah blahing-words the dog has no clue what they mean. For a dog to learn patterns, the human has to show them over and over until they understand. I do not like using the word "command", so I use "ask." However, once they have learned, you only ask them once.

Any fearful or frustrated behavior patterns that where formed at a younger age can be addressed and changed. This goes for the puppy/dog that you adopt or the puppy you might have accidently taught to be defensive. Any fearful behavior can be resolved with consistency and patience. When I say behavior patterns it is not just body language or sound of voice. They also learn the human's heart rate, respiration, energy,etc associated to different action/reactions.

When you are in a sad mood, some dogs may try and force themselves on you to get you stop or see what you are doing. Some dogs are afraid so do not care to be held. Others will nudge the human with their nose to be held and hugged while you cry. They will even lick away tears. How the human responds to the dog's fear or curiosity will set the pattern for the dog to follow. So again during any age period it is important to respond to them the same way every time you are in a different mood. This will in turn teach them how to act in response to your mood energy as they get older. We all have our good days and our bad ones. The way our puppies respond is the way we have taught them or someone else has taught them.

If you are ever in a mood and you are not sure how to handle a puppy/dog situation, the best thing to do is take yourself away from your puppy/dog until the mood/energy passes. Once you are feeling calmer, come back and love on them and let them know all is wonderful. They again may not understand the words being spoken. They will feel the love and the tenderness through your voice, touch, and energy.

If the human desires a confident dog, at any age, expose them to all kinds of different places, humans, and things. The more exposure they have to different sounds, objects, and experiences the more secure they will be. Puppies are full-grown height at 7 months of age. They will continue to body out and go through coat changes until they are 18 months old. So if a dog has fears at this age, they may be able to overpower some humans depending on their breed. A fear-biting Doberman can be a dangerous situation. Here again you cannot blame the dog, though. It is the human family's responsibility to expose and teach them about human family life.

Not exposing a puppy/dog to the world around them would compare to not sending a child to childcare or kindergarten. A child that has not been exposed to social situations may fear going to school and may get in trouble for behavior they were taught at home. Just like an only child, a puppy raised alone may fear another dog taking their toy. This can cause injuries if you ever get another dog or if you take your dog to someone's home that has a dog. It is important to teach your puppy to "release" or "drop it". While teaching, do not keep the toy from them. Just show them what the word/action association is. Praise

Feeding

When first brought home, no matter what age, feed the dog in a kennel or ex-pen. By feeding in a kennel, you will get to see how they behave without outside distractions creating the behavior.

If you have more than one dog, feed them in separate kennels. This will not only prevent fighting, it will also allow you to keep track of if the dog is eating or not and regulate the amount. Also having designated places for them to eat their treats teaches them you have it under control, no fear necessary. All of my family dogs have their beds that they take treats to eat. It is up to the human family to set the patterns and stick to them. Everyone has different feelings when it comes to their dogs. Having everyone in the household understanding the patterns prevents the puppy/dog from getting confused.

If the human teaches the dog they can do as they please, they will. I have heard clients say that the dog will not eat their own food. They have to do something a certain way or else the dog will not eat. Another said they have to put the dogs in separate rooms to feed them or give them treats. These are perfect examples of the dog following patterns of behavior they have **taught** the human. In multiple dog homes you have multiple behavior responses to different situations. Teach new patterns of behavior.

Some humans do not care if the dogs get on the couch. Others feel dogs do not belong on the furniture. No matter what you believe it is up to you to teach the dog and always be consistent in teaching them. Humans allow different patterns of behavior; understand a rescue dog you adopt is set in old patterns. It is up to the new family to teach them the family patterns of living. Be patient and persistent. They will adjust quickly.

If you ever hear someone say they can not do something to the dog, the dog is in control. I tell clients all the time that the dog has taught them very well. Believe it or not, they are not offended. They agree. Of course, some of the things are no big deal to them just as they would not be a big deal to me. However, some humans really let their dogs control the household to the extent that they have to keep their dogs separated all day, every day. This means taking them out separately, feeding them in separate rooms, kenneling them at different times, so they each have some free time. All of this because the dogs have not been taught a different pattern. The human adjusted to the dogs' behavior pattern.

It is human to fear a dogfight because we never want to see our four-legged families get hurt. This is the same when you have multiple children. Fights happen for one reason or another. The way you handle it will be remembered. My parents used to tell us to take it outside and when we were done, they would take us to the hospital if there were injuries. We never did take it outside. We stopped fighting. This is not the best way to handle two or more dogs. It is the human's responsibility to teach the dog they have nothing to fear.

Learning what triggers a fearful behavior response by each dog in the family as well as the children will help decrease fears. It is confusing to the dog to be reprimanded when they are defending themselves. This pattern teaches them to fear who or what they are getting reprimanded for. Multiple dogs in a family feed off each other. A dog that has learned the human's patterns might reprimand another dog, with or without the human right there. I have seen this behavior with some dogs. I said, "leave it" and told them I got it.

Recently, Bailey took it upon herself to help get Faylyn to go outside. I taught all the giant schnauzers in my life to be led by their beard. Faylyn had gotten mud all over her beard, so I was taking her to rinse it off. She planted her feet near the door. I said "Faylyn, come on," when Bailey balanced on her back legs and bopped Faylyn on the behind with her front paws. Faylyn stopped pulling and took a few steps then froze again. I repeated, "come on," and Bailey repeated what she did and Faylyn was ready to get her beard rinsed. I laughed and thanked Bailey for her help. She continues to help when I need it without being asked. ☺

I have had seven dogs at a time and never had a single dogfight. Sure, there was the small growling and warning grumbles, but I never allowed it to go any further. The biggest problem we humans could have is when one dog is pushy of another dog closest to their human. This is when it is up to the human to stop the pushy dog and show them that there is enough of you to go around. If they attempt to attack the other dog, it is up to the human to handle it.

"Harley," rescued Chi MinPin around 4 months old, attempted to attack "Ivy" LC Chihuahua, lying next to me on bed. I gently grabbed her and placed her on her back. I held her in place with my teeth (like mom would) for a second then spit out hair and explained to her that was unacceptable behavior. I did not scream at her or get rough with her. It only took that one time and she never did it again.

"Harley"

Ch Pawfect's I've Got a Secret "Ivy" & "Harley" playing

Really paying attention to your dogs allows you to learn their individual body language. Not all dogs have the same body language. Knowing their body language allows you stop incidents before they happen. You would be amazed how many dogs respond to someone saying, "Do not even think about it." I have said this to so many dogs and some look at me like "What? I was not thinking anything." Others look away from what they were looking at acting like they were not going to do anything. I cannot help but laugh at them and tell them that that did not work I could see they were thinking about doing something. I have even had some look me dead in the eyes and wag their tails as if to say "I would not do that. I love you."

Dogs have learned which family members are the easy targets for getting goodies and fun. So if you want your dog to behave the same with everyone in the household, everyone has to respond to them the same way.

If you do not care how the dog behaves with different family members, then allow everyone to respond the way they want. But remember that the dog will act differently when different family members are around. I had a client who kept the dogs separated all the time. The dogs would get into fights when mom was around. She feared this the most, and they felt it. They did not do this when dad or sis were around because neither of them feared them fighting.

In cases like this, no amount of training by a professional is going to help. It is up to mom to change her ways and do the best to not feel anxious when the dogs are loose together. I boarded these two many times and always kenneled them together and let them out together. They never even growled at each other when they both had a treat in the kennel run. They picked up on mom's nervousness and knew how to get her to respond. When I watched them, they actually became buddies, barking and carrying on at other dogs I was watching.

If something like this is happening at any age and not taught differently there is going to be major problems in the household. The human must take control of the situation or you wind up with a major dog injury. Some humans even say they can not do anything about it and get rid of one of the dogs. To me, that is so unfair to the dogs because the human taught this behavior and now does not want to take the time to rectify their mistake.

Unfortunately, all dogs being rescued and in shelters have some fear-related behavior patterns. Some have run away from home by digging out or climbing out. Others where brought in by their previous humans. Most of them have some kind of behavior problem. Some humans babied and coddled that cute puppy, and now that puppy is no longer cute or cuddly. These dogs are brought to shelters or dumped on the street. Being coddled and babied, these dogs have no social skills at all and will fear everything.

Other dogs that are brought into shelters have been man handled or neglected in some way. I adopted "Magic" a solid black German shepherd 1 ½ years old, when I worked there. Her human brought her in because he did not want to have to deal with her any more. He said he just got rid of her last puppy and did not want her anymore. I guess it was cheaper to get rid of her than getting her spayed. She had to be put in a run by herself because she feared almost everyone and everything. She learned to not fear me and another girl. Everyone saw she was fine with me and her, so we were in charge of caring for her. After a few days, I was approved to adopt her. Once I had her home, she was very protective of the home. She would not let anyone in the fence or in the house if I was not standing next to her.

"Magic"

It was not until I moved that I found out she had a severe fear of men in uniform. She seemed to really get agitated when they had their hat on. As fate would have it, I had a new friend that was in the military and not afraid of her. So he would talk to her and pet her, letting her see he was not going to hurt her. It took a few months, but she did learn that she did not have to fear men in uniforms any more. So no matter how old the dog is or what it has been taught in the past, with love and patience any behavior can be taught to be fearless.

Even though dogs age in years, they stay childlike in maturity. Different breeds mature at different ages. However, I do not think a dog is ever a mature adult like we label some humans. Dogs will always depend on their human family for everything they need until the day they die, so it is up to us to teach them how to fit into our family for their whole life.

If you want a great natural protector, get a female. Though either sex can be taught to protect, it comes naturally for a female. In my multiple dog home, it was the females that alerted and the males just followed along. Others may have different experiences with mixed sexes in the home. It all depends on how the humans act and react when dogs are on duty.

Since you are now dealing with full-grown dogs, you have to teach them appropriate behavior responses to different situations. This especially applies when they have learned they can get away with physical force. If a dog learns they can get away or are allowed to attack another dog with physical force, you have some major issues on your hands. All breeds, from the tiny chihuahua to the largest mastiff will do everything and anything to get away if they are afraid.

You can compare it to a teenage human. They do not want to clean up. They do not want to do their homework. They do not want to go to bed, to name a few. When it comes to stuff like that, they are going to do what they have learned to get out of it. When it comes to things they really want to do, they will beg and try and make deals. Then if not allowed they will get mad and throw a fit and say all kinds of things. The same applies to dogs. Dogs, however, will never tell you they hate you. Their behavior resembles human behavior but coming from fear no other related emotion like anger.

If you do not allow your teenager to get away with this type of behavior, why would you let your dog? Just like humans, dogs desire to live a happy, fearless life. All the dogs in my home learned the patterns of my life. They also learned not all humans in the house will follow through on what they say. I have been told they do things with someone else that they learned not to do with me. Again, if one human allows the dog to do something they know others in the family are teaching differently, the dog will always have the same behavioral response with that person.

This is not fair to the dog because they will do it when this person is around and get in trouble if another family member is around. It's like one parent allowing their teenager to watch TV while they do homework, knowing the other parent does not want them doing that. A teenager, however, can understand that they can only do something while the other parent is gone. Dogs do not understand why they can do something one day and cannot the next. A dog at any age will learn the difference between all humans in their life. But a dog may not be paying attention to which human is the room. Consistency teaches patterns to follow.

I cannot tell you how many times I have looked at a dog and said, "Excuse me." They look at me, and it is like the lights turn on and they realize what they are doing and who I am. Sometimes though they will look at me like "what?" Say "leave it" and praise as they walk away from___. You may also get the ones that will actually trip or do something to make it look like they were not going to do something. Those times you can not help but laugh at them. I have laughed at them and told them they did not fool me. I see what they were doing.

It is like this when they want you to (human terms) feel bad for them. I have seen dogs limp when you accidentally step on their toe. As soon as you are not looking, they walk fine. I watched a dog milk the pity by limping every time the human who stepped on them was looking. They finally stopped when that human surprised them and saw them walking fine. I had a dog that acted like she hated the new puppy when anyone was looking. This went on for days until I caught her playing with the puppy outside. She did not think any one was watching. It was so funny because when she was busted, she wanted to go back to acting like she hated the puppy. I told her that it was too late, that she had been busted. She never played that act any more. She actually played very nicely with him from that point on.

Ch. Rusters Southward Bound "South"
Ch. Skansen's Miss Priss Mar-Vue "Prissy"

So maybe some of you are saying dogs are not smart enough to figure things like that out. I have to disagree. Dogs are by far not dumb. They learn from the humans in their life. Handling so many dogs over the past 38 years, I've seen and learned a lot about them. A lot of dogs' actions are a response to our actions/reactions. Like the dog with the boo boo toe. When the human accidentally stepped on it, they responded by holding and loving on the dog saying they were sorry. Positive loving energy from the human gets repeat behavior.

The dog that acted like she did not like the puppy was also responding to how the human handled the situation. When the puppy would go up to her and mess with her, the human would make the puppy stop and leave her alone. She learned if she behaved like that, the human would step in and stop it for her.

The dog that is afraid of thunder I call storm fretters. They most likely spooked the first time they heard it, and one of the humans picked them up and coddled them. They learn that the human will protect them from that unknown noise. What the human is teaching is that thunder is bad and the dog needs to be protected by a human. Unfortunately, a human will not always be around when there is thunder. That is when dogs dig out of yards and jump out screened windows because they are afraid and have no human to run to for protection. They learned to run to the human every time there is thunder. A dog that is locked up will do what it takes to get to the human. I have seen a dog with such thunder fear dig at a kennel gate until he bled. "Max" was an older yorkie when I moved in with his human. He actually was half dead when I first moved in until he started playing with "Tink," female Jack mix. He got over it when shown that the thunder was not going to hurt him.

Some dogs, however, are not responding to the thunder as much as they are the barometric pressure change. If that is the case, you will see them fretting before a storm even starts. For the ones that are sensitive to the energy (pressure), get their mind off of it by playing with them or giving them a mind toy. The worst thing to do is to coddle them and act like it is something that will hurt them. Most fearful dogs at any age, are only responding to the patterns the humans taught them. Since most puppies are not afraid of thunderstorms. It is a good idea to take them outside during a storm so they can see it will not hurt them.

To me that is very smart. They remember how to act to get specific reactions. How many of you learned how to get a specific response from your parents? We all have, so what makes that any different then what the dog is doing? They are cute and fun when they are young, but they become more challenging as they get older. Does that statement not apply to both children and dogs? We are human. We will make mistakes, but we can fix them as we go along. Be it a child or a dog, if you are teaching them, created and stickto your behavior action/reaction patterns.

Firm/Lenient

I mentioned earlier in the book about things we are strict with and things we can go either way with. Dogs learn the difference between what is sometimes allowed and what is unacceptable behavior. Again it is up to the humans to be consistent so they do not learn something else. You might think a dog is trying you while you are teaching them. They are not. They are learning from you. What you are teaching them is on you. Dogs may not pick up on the word action association behavior you are teaching. They will always learn the associated human action reaction patterns along with the emotional energy involved.

The perfect example is asking them to get off the couch. You tell them "off" multiple times but do nothing. The next time you tell them off the couch, and when they do not, you force them off. Next day on the couch again, you tell them off multiple times but do not follow through. Now they have learned you do not mean it but be prepared to get handled forcefully. Dogs are not stubborn or hardheaded. They have not been taught with clear patterns.

"Shell"

Set Learned Patterns

If you adopt a dog, they actually will be more accepting of change than a younger dog because they do have some life experience behind them. Even though they may have picked up unacceptable behavior patterns or been taught unacceptable behavior patterns, with love and patience, any patterns they may have learned in the past will not be that hard to teach differently. Do not get me wrong. It will take time, but since they were not raised with you, they do not know if you mean it or not. So just like any other age period, if you ask them you have to follow through if you really want them to learn and understand what you are teaching them.

Unfortunately dogs may be defensive. Fear biters learned from their past experiences with humans. Rescue dogs over 7 years of age have had years of abusive handling if they are fear biters. This can be from health issues or living in pure fear of humans. Euthanasia is humane. A single injection and all pain and are fear gone. Their conscious is freed from that body vehicle to continue on their journey. For dogs under 7 and in perfect health, it is best to take it slow and not force anything on them. More than likely, they were treated roughly or not dealt with at all in their previous homes. They will, however, see how the new human handles them and learn accordingly. Once their fear decreases, you can start teaching them the patterns of the household. At times it may be hard to stay calm when they do something, but it is important to talk softly no matter what mistakes they make to trigger past behavior patterns. If you pay attention, you can learn what triggers a specific defensive response/s.

It is different if a dog you have raised has behavior issues. At this point, they have been allowed and taught how to respond to different changes. The only way you change their behavior is to change what you have done in the past. The problem is going to come from other family members. They, too, have learned from the past on how to respond to situations. Every human in the home has to change in the same response.

Dog Behavior Changes

If all of a sudden a dog falls back into an old behavior pattern you have to look at what has changed in your home. Dogs do not just fall back into old patterns for no reason. A dog that has had no accidents in the home since you had it and starts is not regressing. Something is out of pattern for them or they are ill. You have to think back to the first time they did something and figure out what is different.

I have spoken with many clients who have dogs that started doing something they never did or have not done since they were really young. One dog all of a sudden started urinating in the house. After going through a list of things that did not change, the owner figured out what had changed. Her daughter moved in with her small child. She said the dog and the child were always fighting over her attention. The dog's old patterns had changed. What had the human done to start new positive patterns for the dog to live by? I suggested she spend special time with the dog every day without the child around. A few minutes a day goes a long way with a dog.

Another client asked about her dog who started defecating in her home. After going through the routine, she brought up that her daughter had gone off to school. Seems she had been a big part of the dog's life, especially as bed partners. She could not believe that could be it, but she could associate the time she started with the time her daughter left. I suggested she purchase the dog a bed and put it in her and her husband's room so the dog did not feel abandoned.

Sometimes, though, a dog may urinate or defecate in the home trying to show the human there is a problem. Before you get mad look at the accident and make sure it looks OK. A dog I was grooming had an accident when I was getting him out. He had never done that before. I quickly grabbed a mat and put it under him. When he was done, I noticed his urine was full of blood. I, of course, informed his owner and she had him treated. Had he waited until I took him out, I might not have noticed the blood in the grass so well. Dogs will do things to show you something is off.

Dog Communication

Just like a teenage child. Dogs in this age range will talk back when they want something or do not want to do something. To me it is funny to have those types of dogs. It really makes you feel like you have a child in the house. Some have taught their humans well. They learn if they just keep barking or whining the human will give them what they want just to shut them up. Others will bark or whine and then do something cute hoping the human will give in. The key to handle this is to just ignore or tell them it is not going to work. If you give in once, you are teaching that pattern.

Dogs will also lie to you. So do not expect an honest answer if you ask them certain questions. Of course if you ask them if they want to go for a ride, you can believe them bark, tail wag..not ☺. If you ask them if they want a cookie, you can believe them when they wag their tail. Now if you ask them if they did something, they will point their paw at someone else or act like you are playing with them. However, unless you actually saw them do something, you cannot really do anything. This is especially true if you have more then one dog. Some dogs respond fearful, not guilty.

Not sure about the dogs in your home but mine will lie when asked if they have eaten. They will act like they are starving even when someone else in the house fed them. Not only that, they have learned your time schedule and learned when to do things they were taught differently. I know they are called watchdogs, but how do they tell time? It is really funny, though, at day light savings time. They have no idea so it takes time for them to get used to being fed at a different time. I usually do it gradually to help them adjust. They start tapping paw nails one-two hours earlier.

Some humans say they go by the daylight. Others say they are telepathic and can read their owner's mind as they get closer to home. Then you have the ones who say they learned what your vehicle sounds like. It is actually a combination of many things they learned the pattern to.

Some of you by now might be saying I am crazy. However, I bet others are saying they know exactly what I am talking about. If you are one of the ones thinking I am crazy, I ask you to start paying more attention to the dog's behavior associated with different things. A dog is either going to be excited or fearful when the humans come home. Their joyful or fearful behavior will start before the human gets home or as soon as dog hears the car door shut.

Dogs see patterns in everything. If humans would see instead of just look, they would see them also. Do dogs understand time? A dog will be happy to see you if you are gone for just 10 minutes and act like you were gone longer. So even though it could be hours, days, or weeks most act the same. Humans have actually set up video cameras to see what their dogs are doing when they are not home. They see how they start looking for them when it is close to time for human to get home. A secure dog is happy to see you all the time. A fearful insecure dog may have different behavior depending on how long the human is away from them and how they were left. Are they confined, cannot hurt themselves, get into anything or free in house able to tear things up out of fear and possibly get injured?

A dog understands humans a lot faster than humans understand dogs. They also learn patterns to get around things. A dog that has been reprimanded for barking by now has learned how to bark in a way that is not a true bark. "Hope"-LC chihuahua started to sound like a pig because I was teaching her not to bark at everything. Being a happy pacifier she grabbed toys and made her pig noise. It actually was not hard on the ears. I would just tell her "OK, miss piggy."

" Hope"

I have also been around dogs that bark under their breath so to speak. It is like a bark whisper. I have even seen dogs bark without you seeing them move their mouth. You have to give those dogs some credit for learning how to do that. ☺

Dogs learn everything from the humans around them. Humans may find it difficult to teach a different pattern due to their busy schedule. The only way to re-teach a behavior pattern is to be consistent at all times, but sometimes it is impossible to be able to follow through. The dog basically gets away with the behavior. In cases like that, there is no need to get rid of the dog. Get some help from collars, kennels, and playpen/xpens. There is no issue that can not be resolved in one way or another.

When it comes to bringing a dog into your family, no matter what age it is, you have to be willing to deal with all behavior that may come along just like a child. You have to deal with it the best way you can. Sometimes you may have to treat the symptom, not cure the problem. This is also setting a new pattern. Dogs get use to patterns of all kinds.

A dog that has accidents in the house because you do not have the time to watch them can be put in a kennel/playpen. They will have accidents in the kennel and pen until they have learned to hold it and take it outside. If you cannot monitor at all, then a kennel or a gated room is the best solution.

A dog appreciates having their own room/space. It becomes their safe place as long as you never use it as punishment. It is also important not to reprimand them if they have an accident in the kennel /space. By not saying anything, the dog learns they will not get any reaction and they will not like sleeping in the same place they went potty. I have had and watched many dogs that will go to their or any kennel when they are afraid or just want a quiet place. All dogs need their own place. Teaching them their kennel/space is a safe place allows them to go their anytime they feel like it.

As dogs age, the patterns we have created will not just help them. They will also help us spot if something might be wrong. Younger dogs may not understand when a pattern changes. They may act out of confusion. As with any dog, think back to what changed when the behavior first started. All dogs can adapt quickly if the human is consistent with the patterns they are teaching.

In today's economy and society, humans are divorcing, getting jobs, after not working for years or maybe moving. These are all things that could cause any dog to exhibit behavior changes. It is like the dog I mentioned earlier that started defecating in the house when the daughter went to college. For years, this dog was used to the daughter being there and now she was gone. When situations like this happen, it is always good to start a new positive fun pattern with the dog.

Most humans work during the day. Setting a new pattern before work or after the dog will appreciate. It does not have to be active. Something as simple as sitting outside drinking your morning coffee with the dog. This can be very relaxing and love filled for both. Start making special time for you and the dog. The same can be done for a dog of divorce. Since most humans who divorce also have to go to work, the time at home could be less then before. Dogs go through all the stress and worry the human is giving off. I suggest taking the dog to the groomer or some other place away from the moving, something they enjoy and is a normal pattern. Once moved, if you only have one dog, it might help if you let them ride in the car with you, short trips to the convenience store, trips to visit family, any place with the dog, even trips to friends' homes that have dogs they can play with.

Any of the above and a lot of others will work to help them adapt to any changes that arise. Older dogs do not care how many hours you spend with them. Just that you spend some quality time with them. I suggest not starting a new pattern that you may not be able to stick to. You can also change up what you do with them. One day, take them for a walk. The next sit out in the yard with them. I think you get the idea. This way they learn you will do something with them even though it may not be the same every day. Dogs love to spend time with their family members. They love their human family unconditionally. It is important for the human family to do the same.

"Magic"

Nine years and older are pretty reserved. Some may have illnesses the humans in their life caused that will create new behavior patterns. (I do not believe in adopting out dogs over 7 -9 years of age, depending on breed, past and health.) The energy the humans give off affect the dog in all ways. Believe it or not, health issues are caused by negative emotional energy in the household or with main human in life. Test it out for yourself. Look up illness at Our Spiritual Nutrition (link below) and read what the emotional belief is.
http://www.ourspiritualnutrition.com/is05.htm#Our_Spiritual_Nutrition
What are you thinking of when you hold and love on the dog? Do you love on the dog for them or for you?

Most elderly dogs are content to kick back and live the rest of their life without concern. A lot of times it depends on the other dogs in the house. I have seen many older dogs come to life when a younger dog is brought into the home and live a few years more.

During this age period, you sometimes have more to deal with than just behavior issues. This is when dogs start losing their hearing and sight. Younger dogs may act like they can not hear you. I call that selective hearing. Older dogs, though, do start losing some of their hearing. Some may be able to hear high pitches and others low pitches. The ones that cannot hear at all learn to feel vibrations around them. These same dogs may have difficulty discerning voice vibration from other vibrations outside. Do not think they are ignoring you. Tap a pole or a window with a solid ring or something similar to make a different sound/pitch to get their attention. Totally deaf dogs will not hear any sound so they might feel stomping on the ground.

Elderly dogs can scare their humans when they sleep. I can say I have had many that startled me. They slept very deeply, and I could not tell if they were alive. I used to make the mistake of touching them to see if they were still breathing. After scaring the bejeezes out of them, I started staring at their chest to see if they were breathing. It makes your heart skip a beat waiting for their chest to move. I have caught myself holding my breath until I saw them take a breath.

You can always tell when a dog is deaf or going deaf by a change in their bark. I learned the difference in barks from the many dogs I handled over the years. Some deaf dogs began barking more than they did when they could hear. They must like being able to hear something even if it is themselves. I have seen dogs hide their eyes acting like "if I do not see you, you do not see me." I have had dogs of all ages turn away from me and face a wall. Others have tucked their faces in a corner or blanket. OK, so I am being funny now, but it does make you wonder if that is what they are thinking.

For the dogs losing their sight it is important not to do a lot of rearranging of furniture. Dogs learn where things are and will be able to get were they want all the time. I do suggest making ramps for stairs they are used to using. They may be able to maneuver them at first, but as they get older they could misjudge and tumble down. If they get used to ramps before they go totally blind, it will be much easier for them. Dogs that are not going blind during this age can also benefit from ramps.

Older dogs have weaker/brittle bones and joints, like humans. Anything you can do to help them get around better will be appreciated and help prevent injuries. It is helpful for the dog if you keep them at a proper weight. Older dogs have a hard enough time getting up in the morning. They do not need to carry extra weight around. This also applies to dogs with heart conditions. Being over-weight will make their heart work harder than it has to.

Some humans think the dog is starving to death, because they are bony. Be aware that a lot of dogs become a skeleton due to losing muscle. It has nothing to do with not feeding them enough. Over the years I have noticed that you can almost tell a dog is old just by looking at the rib cage. All the older dogs I have been around look as if their rib cage has sprung out. They almost look like they are all ribs. This is because they no longer have the muscle tone that used to fill in their body and legs. If you take away their muscle tone and make them carry more weight, you get a dog that lies around all the time and takes ten minutes just to get up. Because they lie around all the time, they will never lose any weight or build muscle. Lack of exercise equals lack of energy.

Clients have told me that their dog is too lazy and that is why they can not get them to lose any weight. Others have said that the dog is always hungry. They will even bark until they get fed. There is no doubt most older dogs are less active then they used to be. However, feeding them more then they need is not helping them at all. Dogs that teach their owners to feed them whenever they bark are killing themselves. Humans will continue this pattern out of guilt or some other human emotion. The humans in the dog's life have to take their emotions out of it and believe the dog is not starving.

I boarded a dog for years and as she got older, she taught her humans to feed her every time she barked. She, of course, was over-weight and had a hard time walking around. While she was here, she tried that barking trick. It did not work though. The owner told me about her barking for food. I told them she had taught them well. I was aware she had been given the correct amount of food for her size. So instead of feeding her something every time she barked, I took her outside. Because she was so heavy, she would just lie down until I made her walk back in. After a few times of this, she no longer barked. She also lost enough weight in the two weeks she was here that she was able to walk all over the back-yard and really seemed to enjoy herself.

When her humans picked her and her sister up, I told them what I had done when she barked so they would do the same. I also gave them a measuring cup that was marked for how much food she needed to eat. When they saw her, they were very surprised to see how much weight she had lost and how well she was getting around. They were able to keep her weight down from that point until the day she died.

Even though older dogs may be more reserved, they will learn any pattern the humans start. Here again the human has to become aware of the patterns they are creating. Humans sometimes feel bad and want to treat the dog because they are old. You have to be aware that this could start a bad pattern. It is always best to do anything nice when dogs are not asking for it or expecting it. This way they will not associate it with something they have done.

To say you can not teach old dogs new tricks is false. What exactly is a trick? It is a patterned response to an action or sound. Three dogs, golden retriever 3 years old "Phoenix", chihuahua 7 years old "Hope" and chihuahua 12 years old "Tess" all learned what popcorn is popping in the microwave. They have learned it from each other because they sometimes get the last of the bag. To me it is so cute to walk into the kitchen and see all three of them either standing or sitting staring up at the microwave. The 12 year old was the only one that had not learned how to catch it. I do not think she cares, though, as long as she gets some. The other two I think learned how to catch it only because they are pigs and do not want the other dogs to get it. "Hope" and "Phoenix" taught "Faylyn." "Phoenix" and "Faylyn" taught "Bailey."

Older dogs will pick up acceptable or unacceptable behavior patterns. It is false to believe they are too old to learn new behavior patterns. A lot of humans are even easier on older dogs just because they are old (let them behave unacceptably with no consequences). It is not a good idea to do this unless you want them to continue this pattern and any others you create. Older dogs have been around humans long enough to learn just what to do to get the behavior response they desire.

With older dogs, you may have to deal with changes in their behavior when doing things you have done for years. I have handled many dogs, and as they got older they started having what I call panic attacks when being bathed or groomed. These dogs never minded it before, but something seems to snap and they have these attacks all of a sudden. I have seen some panic and start screaming and jumping all over the place. All you can do is hold on to them so they do not hurt themselves until they calm down.

I've had others that just all of a sudden start biting at you. They seem to be unaware of what they are doing. With these you have to avoid getting bit and give them time to calm down before continuing. Some are so bad you have to grab a towel to cover your hands just so you can get your hands on them until they settle down. Then there are those that go into a panic so bad that they start to seizure. Here again all you can do is hold the dog close and talk comforting until they calm and stop seizing.

I have dealt with all kinds of panic attacks and always made sure to let their humans know what they are doing. One of my mom's dogs started to have panic attacks and seizures every time he was groomed. "Duke" was a 14-year-old miniature poodle that started having attacks in the tub. These attacks progressed into seizures, one in the tub and another while he was being clipped. He got so bad that we decided it was best to just keep him brushed out and scissor anything that got out of hand.

"Duke"

The bathtub seems to be the first place an older dog will have a panic attack. It can be very surprising because you are not expecting it. Remember these are all dogs that were fine for years, but now they act like the water is acid. They will start screaming and try jumping out of the tub. Because they are wet they are slippery and so is the tub. The most you can do is try to hold them up so they do not fall and hurt themselves. These old dogs act like they barely have the strength to stand, but in the tub in a panic mode they become very strong.

Another thing about giving older dogs baths is the water temperature. If you ever give your dog a bath and you notice they are swaying and act like they are going to pass out. Turn the temperature down. Older dogs do not always tolerate hotter water. I always have the temperature set the same for all dogs. However, I have to watch it with the older dogs. I've had some start swaying so I quickly made it cooler and cool their heads off first. Once the temperature is fine, they are fine.

As our dogs get older, we also have to deal with health issues that can cause some situations. Besides going blind and/-or deaf, some older dogs become incontinent due to lack of muscle tone. Most of the time the main time this will happen is when they are sleeping. So do not be surprised if you start to see a wet spot where the dog has been sleeping. Here again you can put human baby diapers on them. All you have to do is figure out what size and cut a hole in it for their tail.

"Jay" at 13 years of age was not incontinent but had a lot of "duh" moments. She would just walk into the living and squat and urinate. Newborn diapers fit her just right so when she was out in the living room she wore one. She was not crazy about it, but she got used to it. To me having them wear a diaper is lot nicer than keeping them confined to one room in the house. You can not get mad at them because I do not believe they are doing it on purpose. Dogs get Canine Cognitive Dysfunction (CDD) also referred to as Doggy Dementia or Doggy Alzheimer.

There are no tests for this, but if you have had the dog for a long time you will notice the changes. When I have mentioned to others how the older dog would just stand staring at a wall or into the air, clients have said they noticed their older dog doing the same thing. So if there is anything your older dog is doing that is not behaviorally normal for them, do not be alarmed. Just know it comes with age and you will just have to find the best way to handle it if it is bothering you.

There are natural products that can help older dogs with what ails them. I do not believe in man-made medications because the earth has already provided them.

"Faylyn" is now 10 years old and one of her hip joints has arthritis. I recently had to have the hip rechecked because "Faylyn" had started being incontinent when she slept. The vet put her on rimadyl for pain and suggested I get her some glucosamine to lubricate her joints. When I first found out about her hip. I gave her CBD oil or dog biscuits with CBD. They worked great, but then life got busy and I stopped giving her any.

I used up the Rimadyl before I started her back on CBD oil. I researched glucosamine and found Diatomaceous Earth (DE) food grade is better and earth made. Food Grade: contains 0.5–2% crystalline silica and is used as an insecticide and an anti-caking agent in the agricultural and food industries. It is approved for use by the EPA, USDA, and FDA

I also researched incontinence and natural remedies. Incontinence involves lack of magnesium in the body. There are plenty of foods that contain high levels of magnesium. I picked salmon due to its high levels. "Faylyn's" meals include kibble, DM, CBD oil, dash of garlic powder good for blood (natural antibiotic), fish treat, and water to wet it all. Some meals I add low sodium green beans so they all feel really full without any calories or fat.

"Faylyn" also gets a lot of eye goo around her eyes. To help with her eyes, I shave the hair and eye lashes off around each eye. If you do not feel comfortable doing that, ask the groomer to do it for the dog's benefit.

Chapter Three
Dealing with Death and Dying

No one ever wants to have to deal with the death of the family dog. Unfortunately, though, this is something you have to deal with when you bring a dog into the family. Unlike children, most of us will not out live our dogs. Some humans do make arrangements for the dog if something was to happen to them.

There will be those humans who do not have to decide if and when it is time because nature takes care of that for them. Some humans fear the dog passing when sleeping. I am grateful I did not have to make that choice.

Unfortunately, more times it is up to the human to decide when enough is enough. Many, however, cannot make that decision and try to get someone else to make it for them.

I have seen humans spend all the money they have to keep their dogs alive for themselves. When I am asked how someone knows when it is time, I always replied with "You will know. Let go of the fear emotions and see the whole picture." The problem is not knowing but actually acting on the knowing. A lot of humans know it is time but are afraid they are not looking at it right. They question themselves repeatedly.

Quality of Life

I mentioned in Chapter 1 quality of life in relationship with rescue dogs. What is quality of life and who decides what life quality is? I recently saw a crippled puppy that had been rescued. I asked about it and why. When I was told he has quality of life, I flipped. By whose standards does this puppy have quality of life? Quality of life for the human to get all they want out of them.

It used to hurt my heart when I worked at clinics and saw dogs coming in day after day for some type of worthless treatment. There were a few times the owner asked me if I thought the dog would get better. I had to be honest and told them the best thing they could do for their dog was to take it home. I said make them as comfortable as you can until it is time. So many times humans bring dogs into clinic for treatments, and they are there until they die. How comforting is that for the family dog. They have no one familiar there to be with them. They are in a cage with a towel and water. I will never let one of my dogs be subjected to that cold, lonely death.

I understand humans wanting to do all they can for their dogs. But when does it become about them and no longer about the dog? There is a difference when it comes to loving a dog and keeping it alive because of your feelings. To me, being greedy is not love at all.

I am aware it is heart breaking to let them go, but it is worse to make them suffer just because it will hurt you if they die. I have had to put many dogs down over the years, and it does not get easier. If it was easy, we should not have dogs in our lives. They become a part of the family and no one enjoys losing a family member. However, dogs are not considered family. Humans do have the choice to end their suffering humanely. To me that is the ultimate way of showing them you love them.

Some of you may be thinking that it is not that easy. Think about a family member screaming for more morphine because the cancer pain is unbearable. Being human we want to help, but there is nothing you can do because the law does not allow it. I bet that if the law allowed it, more humans would help family members die just to end their pain. Humans can talk and tell you how much pain they are in and they want it to end. Dogs cannot. It is up to the human family to know them and know when they are saying it is time.

I had a puppy that was born hydrocephalic. "Lucy" was a very happy puppy who never met a stranger. Everyone who ever met her fell in love with her. It was not until she was 7 months out that she started to have problems. She never cried out in pain, but you could tell she was starting to get light and sound sensitive. I would hold her and love on her and it seemed to help. One day though she looked me dead in the eyes with a loving but painful look. At the same time she urinated a little. Right then I told her OK. She did not have to be in any more pain.

"Lucy" could still eat, walk around and go out to go potty. Other than the pain in her eyes and the slight urination, it was not that obvious yet. That was enough for me to witness to know it was time to release her from that body. This loving baby did not deserve to suffer in any way. She was pure love.

"Bouchee" (fawn) "Lucy" (black)

"Tink" was 10 when she ruptured a disc her back. She did everything with me for those 10 years. She would follow me everywhere I went. She and I were best buds. After her injury, she started on medication. However, the pain medication did not seem to help much. The vet I worked for mention surgery. I felt this would cause her more pain then help. I asked to increase the medication and we would see how she did.

"Tink"

For days she was on the medication and seemed to be getting around fine. I took her to work with me every day so I was able to watch and medicate her. One day at work, I took her out to go potty. I thought she was doing fine until she started to walk quickly into the woods next to the clinic. I called her back because she had never gone into that area before. I knew right then that she was not feeling good. I told her I understood and she did not need to run off to die. I took her in the clinic and loved her goodbye.

Dogs will let you know when it is time. It could be like the examples I have written or it could be another way. Knowing your dog and how it acts normally will help you see when they are trying to tell you something. Sometimes you have to just see they are uncomfortable with out them saying anything.

"Jay" was 13 when she started having congestive heart failure. She did well for a few days on medication. But she was having a hard time getting comfortable to sleep. I put a sleeping bag next to the play pen so I could keep an eye on her. I started propping her up in her dog bed with towels so she could both sleep and breathe. This worked for a couple of days. Then she stopped eating and was trying to sleep sitting up. Seeing this, I knew it was time.

Ch Kandee's Simply Pawfect "Tess"
Ch Sonehill's Jade Mist "Jay"
Ch Pawfect-Kandee I've Got A secret "Ivy"

"Hope" was 12 when she started having seizures. I always confine my older dogs in an ex pen to keep them out of things and to be able to check on them. I had walked out of the room when I heard what sounded like her digging at the pen. I went to her to find her in a full grand mal seizure. I grabbed her up and held her until it subsided. It was bad enough to leaving her unsteady for a good amount of time. The second one was days later and was not as bad because I caught it coming on. It was then I said "OK, time."

"Phoenix"

"Hope"

Ch Skyline's Faraona
ES Fabulosa
"Faylyn"

I have never and will never let any dog suffer in anyway. I also will never let a vet tech hold them when it is time for them to go. You do not have to let someone else hold your dog when it is his/her time. Be strong and refuse to let someone else hold them. They can feel your love and will go more peacefully than if a stranger is holding them. Now if you just cannot do it, have someone they know hold them instead. My mom could not do it for her "Duke, so I held him for her.

Another key to knowing when it is time is rating their quality of life. If the dog is still eating, has some spunk and is getting around good, then I am sure they have more time. However, if the dog is lying around all the time, does not respond when they see you, and is hardly eating, then quality of life is gone. I have seen dogs with cancer that do well for months. They are happy and still getting around fine. They are happy to see you and wag their tail to show you. They still have quality of life. Then the day comes when that is gone. They become lethargic and look like a shriveled-up ball of bones. They want to be happy to see you but they just do not have the energy. It is time to end their pain.

I understand some humans feel that if they do not try everything possible then they have failed their dog. Are you sure that it is the dog you are thinking about? When is it enough and when is it too much? Put yourself in their paws. If it was you going through it, would you want your family members to continue treating you or would you want to just go home to spend what time you have with your loved ones? As long as you are having a dog treated for something, they are constantly having to go to the vet to get poked, prodded, and more. I have handled these dogs and feel it is a horrible way to spend what life they may have left.

I know you feel that if you do the wrong thing it will be something you have to live with the rest of your life. I have a million what ifs. If only I had? I should have? The list goes on, and unfortunately it will probably never end. No matter how sure we are, it is only human to question ourselves. All we can do is what we feel is right at the time and know those dogs we have helped are no longer suffering in any way and find comfort in that.

I feel I did what was right for my family members. I did for them what they would do for me if they could. If you are helping your dog suffer less, you cannot question that. Just like they come up and love on you to make your pain go away, just because dogs are not capable of speaking words, it does not mean they are not talking to us all the time. It is just up to us to pay attention and listen.

I am going to end this chapter with "Bouchee."

"Bouchee" came from a litter of three that were c-sectioned. I gave "Boo" to my mom and stepdad when she was 1 year old. Mom became ill so I took "Boo" home with me. One day I could tell she was different but not bad. I spent the day with her pampering her and watching TV and such. The next morning she had passed on her favorite pillow in peace.

Take the time to show them love not fear.

Chapter Four

Professionals

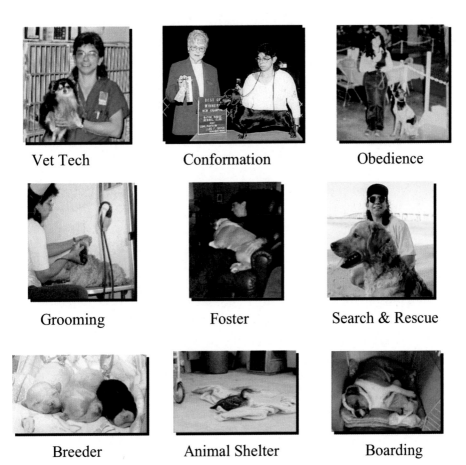

Vet Tech   Conformation   Obedience

Grooming   Foster   Search & Rescue

Breeder   Animal Shelter   Boarding

In my first book "Behind the Doggy Door." I tell of some of my experiences in the different dog fields.

You cannot blame the dog's family for the way they behave with you. It is you and your energy they are reacting to and learning from. The dog can feel your energy as soon as you walk into the room. Understand? They feel you before you touch them. If they are already afraid of your energy they will do all they can to not let you touch them. Failure to get away from you, they now have your hands on them transferring that energy directly. Left hand pulls energy. Right hand sends out energy. What is your energy?

Vet Techs Job

Techs' first and most important job is to not let the vet get bitten. Not only do you have to handle the dog, you sometimes have to handle their human in the room. Having the human in the room makes handling the dog that much harder. If the human feels sorry for bringing the dog to the vet, the dog feels it. If the human hates needles, the dog is feeling it. The list goes on and on.

The tech has the choice to add to it by being afraid of getting bitten or being prepared to show no fear. A dog can feel your energy. How the tech behaves will be the learned pattern or pattern the dog will learn. If you are off in your head thinking negative thoughts, the dog will feel it and go to the learned defensive behavior. If your conscious mind is anywhere other than in that moment with the dog, the dog will feel it. Anywhere you work if you leave all outside work concerns outside, you will be aware of every moment. There is nothing you can do about anything but an emergency while are you at work so why worry. Your feelings are felt by all animals as do you feel all living creatures around you. How many of you have seen a stranger walking toward you and got a bad feeling? That is that human's energy field entering your energy field. Any negative feeling will be felt in a negative way.

Animals are no different. Why does my dog always behave differently with so and so? Their energy is somehow affecting the dog. Someone the dog sees and goes right up to has positive energy (love). Someone the dog tries to bite if they reach for them has negative energy (anger). No matter how you feel about a dog, cat, or human, let it go until they are gone. Dogs learn by patterns. If you are always fighting with them, that is the behavior pattern they learn to expect. Making the whole experience, all the way down to the energy level, positive teaches them it is no big deal and you get a goody. :)

Why Vet Tech

I became a vet tech for the sole purpose of caring for the animals. I had no interest in working politics of any sort. It was not about a title because I am not registered. All that I know about dogs I learned on the job.

Did you become a vet tech because you have a passion for animals?

Did you become one because your family wanted you to?

Did you become one because you thought it would be fun?

Did you become one because of the title and money?

The only correct answer is the first one. If you do not have a passion to work with animals, they will feel it. Passion is love, and all the dogs I handled felt that passion. Dogs are passionate about humans they have no fear of.

Accidents happen when you are off in your head or doing too much at once. One day I accidentally gave a dog a medication, not aware the vet had already given it. As soon as I noticed my error, I went straight to the vet and told her. I asked if she wanted me to induce vomiting. She said yes, and sadly that was why the dog was there. She also told me she was surprised I told her. What does that tell you about the vet tech world? I made a mistake, and I owned it for not just myself but for the safety of the dog.

I have seen so much mishandling by vet techs at the many clinics I worked at. There is such a thing as over handling - all the "registered" techs all around me, yet I was the one called for all the fearful dogs and some cats.

Handling

Brute force is never needed to restrain a dog or cat. By forcefully restraining a dog you are giving them something to fight with. Vet techs are taught anatomy, but how many can hold a dog because they understand it? There are so many ways to hold a dog without brute force but still have control. By staying calm, feeling only love, and only using the pressure necessary to hold them, teaches animals it will be done without a fight and it does not hurt. They have nothing to fear.

Is this a reaction controlled out of understanding and being prepared or reaction out of fear? Fear reaction will trigger a fearful dog into a learned defensive behavior filling the whole room with negative human emotional energy.

As I mentioned human hands transfer energy directly. As long as you do not break that connection all will go well. The left hand, if the tech is relaxed, will draw off fearful energy and the right hand will give them positive loving energy to replace it. When you focus everything about you on the dog you create an energy bubble around the two of you. The tech is teaching the dog, they care and would not cause them any harm. Can you picture that calm moment? Now picture the tech irritated about something out of their control. That frustrated energy handling an already fearful dog will not go well. Why do that to the dog? You are there for them and nothing else matters.

OK, that is handling the dog now to handling their human or humans. :)

Animals' behavior and health are a reflection of the human/s emotional states in their life.

I was called to handle a chihuahua for a family visit. Everyone else was afraid to reach in and get her out of the kennel. How many of you have dreaded a dog coming in? How many are afraid of that little piranha chihuahua? LOL, guess what? They feel it before you even touch them. Because of that they will not let you touch them.

When I walked in the room with her family, mom was all gushy, her baby. I told her, yes, she sure is and her behavior reflects it. Her husband and son both said, "Told ya" LOL. Not only that, I am now aware that her health was also an effect of her being her baby. Dogs do not have an ego so they do not have negative feelings, only fear. It is those negative emotional energy feelings that eat at the human as well as any living creature around.

Keeping an animal alive for your selfish reasons is inhumane. Humans bring a dog in for treatments that could be done at home are really only delaying the inevitable. When I get the chance, I have a little chat with them. :) I tell them I can see they love them very much and I am sure they love you. How would you feel not having much of any quality of life left and being taken here there and such? Hospice-would you not be happier at home spending the time you have left with the ones you love not doctors and nurses? Home is filled with love not at a noisy clinic filled with illness.

A Show Handler's Job

Handlers' first and foremost job is to care for the dogs they have been hired to handle, not only at their facility but also on the road. The show world looks all glamorous and such, but looks are deceiving.

I have seen handlers kick, hit, pull ears, etc. How is that caring for the dog? The dog's behavior is all on you, so get mad and hit yourself. You have taught that dog your pattern of behavior associated with your negative emotional energy.

Politics aside what do you have? Dogs are living, loving creatures that did not ask for this. The humans in its life chose it for what? If it is about having fun teaching the dog and showing them off, that is positive. Unfortunately, most humans are not doing it for that purpose, and it is the dogs that suffer.

An Obedience Trainer's Job

Like show handling, obedience trainers are entrusted to take care of a family dog for weeks. Why are you teaching a dog to be obedient? How many homes need an obedient dog? The average family home will not ever show the dog in obedience, so that training is worthless.

You do not train someone to dance you teach them.

Stop training obedience and start teaching the dog the English language. Teaching tools required to teach a dog anything: love, lead, martingale collar and flirt pole (to work body and mind before class). Dogs learn patterns. They learn when they have a shock collar on, pinch collar anything other than I listed. They are only Band-Aids because when you take them off, the behavior is still there.

Are you teaching the dog to love the human or teaching them to fear them? I have been around enough so-called professional trainers, and honestly they are not professional nor do they teach the dog with love. Alpha/pack leader garbage is what most teach, which is ca ca. A dog trained to fear is living a life in fear. A fearful dog is a ticking time bomb that the human created.

A Groomer's Job

Grooming is not just about making dogs beautiful, it is about a whole lot more. A groomer's job is to take other human created balls of fear and make them look beautiful in only so much time. A groomer has to re-teach the English language to almost every dog that comes in. "No moving or stop moving" means stop whatever it is you are doing because this will be done and it is not hurting you. "Stay or be still" means do not move a muscle or I might nick you.

Then there are the silent lessons. As soon as you stop pulling, I will continue doing what I am doing, I will not let go before then. Most dogs that bites have learned that it is the action to take to set themselves free. They do not bite hard, but most humans will jerk their hand away. This is the action reaction a dog learns so we as groomers have to control our instinctual response to jerk away from possible pain, to see if they are serious or just warning/testing to see if human will let them go. Once we have established why they are biting, we adjust. Warning bites will eventually stop when they see your response is not going to be to let go.

Some dogs find it fun to continue to test, but it is harmless. I just tell them they are being funny. For the ones that have so much fear they are lashing out and could hurt you, it is time for an e-collar or leather gloves (not tight on your hands) or both. Let me add no noose or muzzle because this will only reinforce the dog's fearful behavior. You cannot reinforce fear but you can a behavior they learned.

A groomer also has to show/teach dogs that a dryer is not a beast from hell coming to kill them. Show/teach them it is just water not acid. Show/teach them that the buzzing thing in our hand just sounds scary but is really harmless if they are still. Show/teach them that their nails have to be cut so they can walk on their pads. Show/teach them we have to pull the hair out of their ears so they can hear better and the ear can breathe. After all this, the human family asks how you where able to do something because the dog will not let them.

Once you stop laughing you can tell them that you are a groomer who understands why a dog behaves the way it does, and changing the way you respond changes their actions. Negative (fear-based) responses to negative reactions produce more negative responses. Positive loving responses to negative action (fear-based) will lessen the fear. There is so much more, from dogs that submissively urinate to cage fear and one of the worst is fear of touch. You touch them and it is like you are shocking them every time the way they react. All of this is a road map of how they are being taught the human language at home and the results of specific actions they have learned from experience. Do not blame the dog. It is only doing what it has learned from his or her human family.

Grooming is not hard if you understand a dog's behavior and learn how to handle different situations. When I say learn how to handle, I mean without nooses, muzzles, slings, etc. Using force of any kind on an already fearful dog will only validate their fearful behavior and creates more. Wearing a single fitted leather glove is all you need until they see you are not going to hurt them, even if they bite you. For a severely fearful dog, a soft-sided e-collar helps and is none restraining. If you show fear, you will receive a fearful reaction from the dog. Being prepared has no fear.

*Note:- A dog you know will bite when getting their nails cut never do it alone. A dog that is afraid will take a while to teach differently. Holding the dog off the table in your arms, your leg propped up for heavy or really strong dogs, and having someone else cut the nails teaches it will be done without a fight. For large breeds, try a grinder instead of clippers. Everything you do teaches the dog an association. If you use a noose and muzzle, you are teaching the dog that you are going to cut their nails, choke them and put something around their mouth. That is the pattern the dog has learned happens every time they go to the groomer. If that was you, would you want to go back? Would you want anyone touching your nails?

Avoid a lot of situations with something as simple as a table placement. A table out in the middle of a room is dangerous for the dog. A lot of groomers like their table that way so they can walk around instead of having to turn the dog around. Those groomers only have themselves to blame for a dog that acts out, because the dog has 360-degree fear factor radius around them.

Picture standing on a table, at least three feet off the ground, with a pole right in front of you and open space to your left and rear with the groomer standing on the right side. A fearful dog has four places they have to guard, so they will be reacting to things going on around them. Placing a table against a wall decreases the fear factor to 75percent. Placing your grooming equipment to the left or right of the table brings it down to 50percent. There are only two places the dog has to be aware of now. Not using a noose will reduce it even more and with only two ways the dog could get away from you, there is no need. The dog will always be aware of you because you are touching them and you will be aware of them.

Groomer Helpers Not Dog Helpers

If your dog severely fears going to the groomer, find another groomer. There are devises (tables, slings, etc.) being sold as groomer helpers. Think about this. Anything that helps the groomer does not necessary help the dog. Noosing a dog up so it cannot move is torture for the dog. Slinging a dog up so it cannot move is torture. Muzzling and noosing a dog is torture. None of these devices are necessary when you understand dog behavior and show love and understanding when handling them.

How do these groomers expect the dog not to be afraid if they continue to validate the torture every time the dog gets groomed? The ONLY way to teach a dog it has nothing to fear being groomed is to show them without restraints. If you cannot handle a dog without torture devises, then maybe you should not be grooming dogs.

If a groomer calls themselves a professional, they are supposed to be able to handle any dog without any special devises. A leather glove and maybe an e-collar are all they may require. They are helpful for BOTH without added fear.

Stop paying for your dog to be tortured. Do a little research on the so-called groomer helper devises your groomer has in their shop. If the grooming tables are not against a wall, which I feel cuts down on the dog's fear, the groomer can add a false wall as pictured in the photo. This wall prevents the dog from falling off that side as well as relieving the dog of having to guard that side from attack.

Table wall

Grooming certificates only say that groomer knows how to groom the hair (breed pattern) not handle any dog without restraints. I have offered to teach how to handle for free but have had zero inquires from anyone. As long as humans continue to pay for their family dog to be tortured, the more it will be normal practice at grooming shops.

When you understand everything about the dog and some cats speaks of the emotional environment they live in. You can see how your energy can either be a part of their emotional environment or a positive change from it.

I could go on and on but will end by saying your emotional energy affects everything around you. These animals are already afraid of having to be there. Please do not be one who validates their fearful behavior. Live in each moment, not off in your head, showing them instead there is nothing to fear and that fearful behavior is unnecessary.

A Foster's Job

Humans took me from my canine family to a new home. I was very young, cute, and cuddly. It took me time to understand what those humans asked of me. This made them mad, and they locked me up all the time. I did figure out what the house patterns were for me. My hair was fluffy and required brushing to not get matted. The humans kept me brushed out for the first few months of my life. Little by little, I was no longer so cute and cuddly. The human contact became less and less.

Years past and the humans would have me shaved naked once a year. It felt good to have the weight of matted hair removed and to be able to get to my skin to scratch. After the hair cut, I also got to spend time in the house. Once my hair got long and started to get dirty, I had to live outside by myself. The day came when someone left the gate open, and I walked out. I spent days on the streets covered in my heavy matted hair that I could barely see out of. My health had been going down for a while, but the humans did not care.

Living on my own was not easy, but I did find some food and places to sleep. When I came across humans, they would chase me off or stay far away from me. One day as I was eating some tidbits from a trash bin, a man in a uniform came up and talked to me. I was very scared and I had a hard time hearing and seeing him. I tried to hide behind the bin but he was able to loop something around my neck. I walked with him to his truck where he picked me up and put me in a square section and closed the door. I became even more frightened as it made a sound and began moving.

After some time we stop moving and the man opened the door and carried me into a room. There another human came up and looked all over me pushing and pulling. They tried to see under the matted hair but it was too tight. Another human came in and started shaving off my matted hair. It was uncomfortable for me in places, where the hair cut into my legs. At the end I was cold but lighter. I could see everything and everyone not sure what was going to happen next.

That is just one experience that a shelter dog may have. As a foster, you have to take all of that into consideration. Bringing a dog home and letting it loose in an unfamiliar setting is not going to reduce that dog's fears. Kenneling them and finding out what type of toy they like. The last three fosters I had in my home all went to their new home with THEIR toy.

"Milo" ("Milo" and "Mason" journeys last chapter Understanding Behavior) was very frustrated and liked to chew things up. I found toy he could chew on as hard as he desired. "Mason" was scared of everything and enjoyed a chew dispenser toy. "Pete" had no frustration-just afraid-has a stuff-less fox toy. Every time they were kenneled their toy was put in there with them. If they were out with it, no other dog was allowed to take their toy. "Pete" does enjoy playing tug with "Bailey."

"Bailey"   "Pete"

As a foster, your job is to care for that dog in your home until it is ready for adoption. Caring for includes and is not limited to feeding/watering, shelter, and safety from other dogs or humans and teaching them proper English word action association with love.

Search and Rescue's Job

You have to teach a dog for search and rescues. They will not understand what you are asking unless you show/teach them.

I was head instructor for one county, but the members had no desire to teach the dog. Was it because I was a woman and they were all men? Whatever the case, the friends I brought in decided to start our own in another county. We taught the dogs land and water search and got all our dogs certified for land.

Just because someone went on a search and claims to be a SAR K-9 unit does not mean they are. I heard of a vet claiming this but never taught a dog nor did they send a dog out. From what I was told, they only attended a search. All of our team carried these cards with us on all searches.

Human and animal lives are at stake here. False claims can cause more pain and suffering.

A Breeder's Job

Breeding is more than taking a male and female and putting them together. Genetic conditions are something you must take into account when breeding. There are tests that can be performed to rule out some conditions so not to double up on it.

A dog can be a carrier of a condition and show zero signs of it. It is those dogs that if tested the breeder would be able to avoid breeding to another carrier creating the condition in the whelps.

Breeding is not about the money humans can make but about the improvement of the breed. It is not just about how they look but also their health. Unsanitary environments are not about the betterment of the dog/breed. It is about the human making money. Just because a female normally goes into heat every six months does not mean to breed them every time. Breeding a dog every heat takes a lot out of them and if they are not cared for properly could kill them. How would you like being pregnant or caring for a baby your whole life?

A family says they are only breeding the family dog so the kids can experience it. If that is your excuse, I hope the children are also ready to deal with death and possible heart breaking situations.

If humans did not make any money off breeding dogs how many would still do it?

A Shelter Employee's Job

Dogs that come into a shelter are going to have some fear of the unknown as well as fear of the experiences it might have already had with humans. How you handle them will either increase their fearful behavior or decrease it.

Kennel techs and officers have different jobs.

An officer's job is to go out on calls of all kinds involving animals. No matter what species they are going out for, those animals will have fear. It is up to that officer to obtain that animal. How they do this depends on each situation.

When other humans are involved, it becomes more dangerous. A dog's human being there will affect the dog's behavior according to what that human has taught them. I am not talking about attack training. I am talking about the human emotion action/reaction. If the dog's human is feeling any negative emotion that dog is going to behave according to the patterned emotional response that human taught them.

The officer has to be aware of everything around them at that moment. If that officer is all wrapped up in their own fear/anger, they could get hurt. Officers get attacked by dogs all the time. All the ones I am aware of involved human family members being present.

Stray dogs have only the fear of the human and that depends on how humans in their past treated them. Some will actually go straight to the officer. They have tried to go other humans but they shooed them off. It only takes a few minutes to show a dog you will not hurt them. It is a big scary world out there.

Working at a shelter you see all kinds of humans and dogs. You can learn a lot about both if you turn off your emotions and see them. A human's behavior and a dog's behavior are no different. A defensive human and a defensive dog are AFRAID. A human parent teaches their children and a human parent teaches the dog. When you turn off your own human emotions you do not feed into theirs. Getting angry with either only validates the defensive behavior and accomplishes nothing but total negative energy filling the room. Now all the dogs and humans around feel it.

Working at a shelter for me was hard only due to humans I had to deal with daily. Some of these humans I never met, but seeing what they did to the dog was enough. As an employee, it is your job to handle all kinds. If you see them and see how the dog behaves you begin to understand it is the human to blame not the dog. Treat the dogs with love and compassion. Treat the humans with respect until they have left. Then you can scream and all that stuff to get it out.

Boarding Kennel Attendant's Job

This job is no different than a trainer or handler when it comes to the human entrusting you with their family dog. With boarding, all you have to do is teach the dogs the pattern of the facility. Keep them fed, watered, and exercised and maybe groom or bathe them before they go home. Some dogs have medication you have to administer and monitor. The only other thing is cleaning the living area.

The different types of kennel set ups can make it hard to clean with a dog in a run. If you have to clean with a dog in the run and they have nothing to jump up on, do not use a sprayer and get the dog wet. It is just as sanitary to pick up the poop and then mop. Using bleach and other chemicals on the floor more than just mopping can burn the dog's pads. I have seen plenty of dogs with chemical burned pads getting groomed after being boarded.

Until a dog has learned the pattern of the facility, it may exhibit fearful, defensive behavior, it is up to the humans involved to teach them that all is wonderful and they have nothing to fear. Do you mix families' dogs to exercise? Do the kennel attendants understand canine behavior in a real sense? How many dog fights have there been in the play yards? Were there any injuries? It only takes one dog screaming just the right way to set off all the rest of the dogs in that area. You will have the ones that run in fear and you will have the ones that get fired up. You have humans screaming and such only raising the fear energy out of control.

When I boarded dogs, I might let out two families of dogs. Two dog's one family plus one. I am one human. I can only teach a small number of dogs at a time. It takes time to learn a dog's behavior triggers, which you can learn with dog-to-dog interaction through a fence. A fence prevents contact fights and can aid you in teaching the dog proper behavior for fun time.

When you understand a dog's behavior is a reflection of the humans in their life, do you want to be another human the dog fears or change your action/reactions to more positive loving ones?

Dog Field Employees

As someone who has worked in almost all dog fields, I can say humans are to blame for all negative dog behavior. Why did you get a job working with dogs when you could care less about their well being? You say "I do care." If that is the case, why do dogs frustrate you or why are you afraid of them?

I was mauled by a chow shepherd mix and still went on to handle all types of behavior without getting bit. That story is in my first book, but if I did not have a passion for dogs that would have done it for me.

If you work in any dog field, you will get bitten. The severity of the bite will depend totally on you. No matter what you do in life, when you learn to not emotionally react, life is a lot more positive. Be prepared for anything. Your reaction is then a planned response to a specific action. When you are off in your head, thinking about anything, you cannot respond as planned. A fumbled, mindless reaction can start a rollercoaster of action reactions.

All that you do to a dog teaches them who you are. Anger is fear and that the dog learns very quickly. Everything about the human is learned by every dog they handle. If you always have a hard time handling dogs, then it is time to take a deep look at yourself. They are behaving according to what you taught them about your energy associated behavior.

Dogs give unconditional love. Why can't humans give back the same?

At the young age of 5, I knew my life would involve animals. I was raised with horses, a cat, and dogs. I thought I wanted to be a veterinarian when I grew up. But as I got older and being raised with many animals, I was not sure if I could be a vet. I did know I would work in the animal field.

When I was 16, my parents divorced and my mom needed help. She said she did not care what job I got, as long as I got work. I knew I was not just going to do just anything. A friend of mine knew I wanted to work with animals and told me about a pet grooming shop that was hiring by her house.

That was my first job working with animals. Here I learned grooming, training, breeding, and whelping. As the years followed, I worked at many grooming kennels and also got experience as a veterinarian technician. As a technician I worked at different clinics including emergency and specialty clinics.

Having grooming experience, I was able to get involved in dog showing. I worked for two of the top handlers in my area in the '80s. Both taught me handling and grooming skills that I was grateful to learn. I taught grooming at a grooming academy and a community college.

With my training experience, I got a job working for a few Greyhound racing kennels including one breeder kennel. It was an experience I never want to have again. With kennel and vet tech experience, I qualified for a job at the county animal shelter where I lived. There were lots of heartaches to experience there. This was where I truly learned how evil some humans can be when it comes to their pets and how they treat them. After that I went back into a grooming/training/handling business with a partner and I got the pleasure of being head trainer of our county K-9 search and rescue team. The whole team received a certification for land search with their dog by a certified search and rescue trainer/author.

Today I can groom all fearful small, medium, and some large breed dogs without a noose or muzzle, just one leather glove. I can scale teeth without sedation just by laying the dog in my lap. All dog behavior is a reflection of the type of human interactions they have had. It is not about obedience but working together with compassion and love. All we are doing is teaching a foreigner the English language. How we do that is what makes a difference.

All of my knowledge/wisdom is from experience not from a book/ books I read. What I speak of and teach is simple, easy- to- understand information, from personal experience. My long-term goal is educating the masses by offering speaking engagements.

Made in the USA
Middletown, DE
28 March 2022

63218740R00055